WH...

PARENTS
ARE DRIVING
YOU UP THE WALL
AND WHAT
TO DO
ABOUT IT

PENGUIN BOOKS

UK | USA | Canada | Ireland | Australia
India | New Zealand | South Africa

Penguin Books is part of the Penguin Random House group of companies
whose addresses can be found at global.penguinrandomhouse.com.

www.penguin.co.uk
www.puffin.co.uk
www.ladybird.co.uk

First published 2019

001

Text copyright © Dean Burnett, 2019
Illustrations copyright © Katie Abey, 2019

The moral right of the author and illustrator has been asserted

Text design by Mandy Norman
Printed in Great Britain by Clays Ltd, Elcograf S.p.A.

A CIP catalogue record for this book is available from the British Library

ISBN: 978–0–241–40314–3

All correspondence to
Penguin Books
Penguin Random House Children's
80 Strand, London WC2R 0RL

DEAN BURNETT

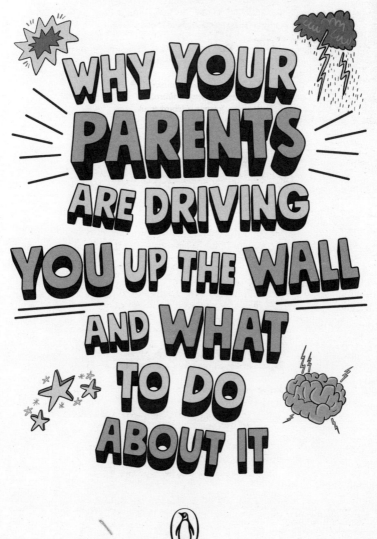

WHY YOUR PARENTS ARE DRIVING YOU UP THE WALL AND WHAT TO DO ABOUT IT

PENGUIN BOOKS

Dedicated to Sian and Peter Burnett, my own parents.

When I wrote this book,
I promise I WASN'T thinking of you.
Much.

CONTENTS

WHO IS THIS BOOK FOR?

DO YOU HAVE PARENTS? IF SO, THIS BOOK IS FOR YOU.

Hang on, of course you have parents. Unless you're reading this in the future and they've worked out some way of making people from scratch. Probably with robots.

Let me start again.

Are you a twenty-first-century person, made by human parents in some version of the traditional (let's not go there) way? And can these parents be literally the most annoying people in the world ever?

If so, this book is for you.

Have you found yourself arguing with them recently about pretty much every-thing? Is this stressing you out?

In this book, I'm going to tell you – Hang on. I should introduce myself.

WHO I AM

Hello, I'm Dean, and this is my book.[1] Yes, it really was – and that comment only makes sense if you've had a look at the footnote. Please do have a look at them. They're worth checking out![2]

Technically, my full title is 'Dr Dean Burnett', but if we ever meet in person it's just 'Dean', honestly. If you're holding one of my books, I've no business getting all snooty.

I really am a doctor, though. Not a 'say ah, let me look in your ear' type doctor. I've got a PhD, or doctorate, which is what they give you when you spend a really long time learning about one thing. For me that was neuroscience: the study of the brain and nervous system. Basically, I'm a doctor of brains.[3]

---

1. Well, it's *yours* really. But it was mine first.

2. You never know what you might find here.

3. The human brain is the most complex object in the known universe. I'll leave you to decide if being a brain doctor is the best kind of doctor, rather than, say, a doctor of feet. Or gums.

I've learned a lot about the human brain, so much so that I've ended up writing books about it. Like the one you're holding now. However, this book isn't like my previous ones. This one is better, because it's not for adults. It's for someone more interesting. You.

WHO YOU ARE

I should probably say, I'm assuming that you are a human adolescent. An adolescent is anyone in an 'intermediate' stage of development, between child and adult. This stage seems to be starting earlier with each generation, and at present it begins at age 11 or 12. You can trust me on this – I'm a science person.

But 'adolescent' isn't a word that we use every day – most of the time people talk about children, teenagers or adults. So, in this book, when I refer to 'teenagers', that includes 10- to 12-year-olds too. Because, scientifically speaking, people that age are teenagers, 'adolescents'. It's not the label that's wrong; it's numbers. They should go: 'seven, eight, nine, tenteen, eleventeen, twelveteen, thirteen . . .'[4]

But this book is specifically meant for those of you aged between 10 and 16. Obviously anyone and everyone can read it, but if you fall into that age range, welcome!

Everything that follows is **especially for you**.

---

4. They get it right in some other languages – look at what French does for instance: *onze, douze, treize* – no difference between 11 and 13!

PARENTS VS TEENAGERS

This book is unusual because it's about the relationship between teenagers and their parents.

Now, that's not actually an unusual subject for someone to write about, but the millions of words in the other books, articles, resources, leaflets and websites about the teenager–parent relationship are written *for parents*, and explain how to deal with their oh-so-difficult teenage offspring.

This book, however, is for *you*, and explains how to deal with *your difficult parents*.

Because let's face it: they can be impossible. It can often feel like there's not a single area of your life they don't have a wrong opinion about – from how you spend your time to who your friends are and how you communicate with them.

They can give you a hard time even when you're not in

a good mood about something! So they want a say in your actual feelings!

You've probably noticed that you've been disagreeing with and resenting your parents a lot more than when you were younger.

It's as if, after years of being reliable, they've suddenly started malfunctioning.

So I guess what you probably need is a user's manual to understand what's going on.[5]

'SO WHOSE FAULT IS IT THEN?'

Well, nobody's really.

The first thing to say is, there's nothing *wrong* with any of you. Teenagers and adults butting heads is a fact of life. One of the earliest recorded examples of

---

5. That's basically what this book is!

an adult moaning about 'kids today' can be found in the writings of Socrates, the ancient Greek philosopher who lived around two and a half thousand years ago.

What he said was:

> THE CHILDREN NOW LOVE LUXURY; THEY HAVE BAD MANNERS, CONTEMPT FOR AUTHORITY; THEY SHOW DISRESPECT FOR ELDERS AND LOVE CHATTER IN PLACE OF EXERCISE.

Sounds familiar, right? All that's missing is:

> THERE IS TOO MUCH TIME SPENT ON THE BOXES OF X AND STATIONS OF PLAY.

Clearly, teenagers like you have been arguing with parents for thousands of years. The real question is . . . why is it automatically *your* fault? Why is it *you* who needs to be managed, dealt with, handled, or any other word that makes it seem like you're the one in the wrong?

BIG DEAN REMEMBERS LITTLE DEAN

This is something that's bugged me for a very long time. Because, like every other adult on Earth, I was once a teenager myself. And while your teens are always a confusing, chaotic and stressful time, what with all the changes going on in your body and brain, I remember there were plenty of things I was told that seemed inconsistent, or just plain unfair.

I would occasionally mention this to my parents, teachers or any other adult who'd listen, and what did they say? 'You'll understand when you're older.'

But here's the thing: I *am* older now, and have spent a large part of my life reading loads of stuff. And I *still don't understand*!

How can teenagers be 'withdrawn' and 'self-obsessed', right up until you feel passionately about an issue, at which point **you're 'naive' and 'melodramatic'**?

You almost always know more about the latest technology than your parents, but they get to set the rules on how it's used? Based on something they read in a newspaper, written by some other even older person who clearly hasn't got a clue, just an opinion?

I worked incredibly hard at school. Mostly because I felt like I *had* to, seeing as I was told repeatedly – by parents, teachers and the rest of the world – that good marks in exams were vital if I wanted to have *any* chance in life. And then exam results were published, and, like many other teens around the country, I got good marks. And what was the first thing I saw on TV that day? Politicians, on the news, bleating that

EXAMS ARE TOO EASY!

Constantly tell us we're doomed if we fail our exams, but insist we must be dumb if we pass! Brilliant. Cheers. That's quite a confidence boost. The list goes on.

Teenage Dean may now be pushing forty, balding, overweight Dr Dean, but these gripes never went away. My younger self is still in there somewhere, fuming about the injustice of it all.

Luckily, dedicating my career to learning how the brain works does mean I now understand a lot more about how and why teenagers and their parents butt heads so often. And that understanding is what I hope to share with you in this book.

SURPRISE, SURPRISE – IT'S YOUR BRAIN

A lot of it comes down to the workings of your brain. Even though you share the same house, and even the same genes, your brain works in very different ways to those of your parents, at the most fundamental levels. You think about things differently, perceive things differently, react differently, prioritize differently. Is it any wonder that you regularly don't see eye to eye? Often, you literally *can't*.

And these differences show up in many ways, causing numerous arguments. This book is built around some of the most well-known and persistent ones, and will hopefully give you some insight into why you do what you do, why your parents do what they do, why issues occur and, particularly, what you can do to avoid them.

This is important because your brain is still developing,

undergoing massive and rapid changes. This is very good in many ways, but it also means that it's often more vulnerable to disruption and stress. The mental health and well-being of teenagers is a crucial issue in today's world, and stress and anxiety are major factors in this.

But one of the key elements of your young life is the relationship you have with your parents. **So the less hassle there is, the better.**

And that's where this book comes in. It's impossible to avoid arguing with your parents entirely, because it's just a fact of human life. But maybe, by learning why your parents think and act as they do, and why it's so different to what *you* think and do, you can better understand where they're coming from, and avoid the more predictable conflicts and frictions that add needless stress to your already stressful existence.

Because the truth is parents often feel like you just don't get it when they talk to you, so any attempt you make will almost certainly be gratefully received. Because they definitely weren't given a definitive instruction manual when you were born. They're just muddling through, desperately reading parenting books, talking to friends, trying to work out how to actually be a parent. Most of the time they probably feel like they're making it up as they go along.

Just making an attempt to understand where they're coming from will probably make for an easier life for all concerned . . . Can't hurt, anyway.

And, yes, technically it shouldn't be your responsibility to deal with all this. But it's either that or leave the adults to handle it. And that's how we ended up here to begin with!

BEFORE WE GET GOING

Before we go any further, let me just say a couple of important things.

I obviously don't *know* you, your parents or what the relationship you have is like. These things are so different for everyone that I couldn't *possibly* know. But I've had to make some assumptions or generalizations when writing this.

I've used descriptions like 'parents' and 'mum' and 'dad' when I'm talking about the people in your life who you might want to understand a bit better (something this book might be able to help you with).

Of course, there are lots of different shapes of family. You might have an adopted mother or father, or step-parents, or just one parent, or two dads, or two mothers, or live with your grandparents or siblings. Pretty much everything in this book will be just as relevant to you: I just refer to 'mum' and 'dad' to save time and avoid phrases like 'parental unit' because that's just creepy.

Another assumption I've made is that you have a normal or typical relationship with your parents, as far as teenagers are concerned. You still *care* about each other, your parents still have your best interests at heart, but you're arguing a lot more lately, about so many things, and it's starting to get to you.

Unfortunately, teenagers can have relationships with their parents that *aren't* typical, in very unpleasant ways. Abusive, toxic, hostile relationships between teenagers and parents are sadly quite common, but not something I'm able (or qualified) to get into here. There are some helpful resources at the back of this book though, if you think you're in such a situation. If even a tiny part of you wonders if you are, then please do find someone to talk to.

And finally, you might read a lot of what follows and think, *That's not something that happens to me!* In which case, good. Not every teenager argues with their parents. Some never do.

Everyone is different, and no book ever written can be applied to everyone equally.

But just because some parts don't apply to you, it doesn't mean none of it will. And it may become very relevant later in your life. Who knows? There's also still plenty that explains what's going on in both your parents' heads and yours, so maybe by reading this you'll be able to *avoid the problems I mention altogether*?

CHAPTER 1

'YOU TREAT THIS PLACE LIKE A HOTEL!'

>>>FAULT: Parents are making a big deal out of small things and ignoring how the teenager feels.

HAVE YOU EVER HAD A SHOWER?

I'm guessing the answer is 'yes' (baths also count).[6]

Well, have you ever showered, then left your wet towel on the floor? Or your bed? Or anywhere other than **the place the towels belong**?

If you have, it's totally understandable: after a shower you're damp, cold, and don't have any clothes on. Nobody likes that feeling, so the main thing on your mind is dealing with that, not worrying about the location of a towel. So, you put it down, you forget about it. It happens; we all do it.

However, I'm guessing your parents don't feel quite the

---

6. I realize this is very early in our relationship to suggest you're smelly.

same about the whole towel thing? Maybe they've even yelled at you about it? A lot?

What is *going on* here? Has their 'reasonable response' system short-circuited? Is it a glitch that means they see every minor, harmless oversight as a world-ending disaster?

Because it's not just towels, is it? A misplaced sock, a briefly uncleared plate or cup – all this and more can result in you being yelled at. Why? It's mostly stuff that can be dealt with in seconds. None of this feels *important*. It's not like you're doing anything to *deliberately* upset them.

Of course, if you try telling your parents that, they just get angrier and yell more.

This is clearly unfair. So, you get angry back at your parents, for always having a go. For always taking that specific tone they do, like you're the worst person who's ever lived, when you know that other kids are actually far worse than you.[7] Then they accuse you of being melodramatic *and* of being ungrateful and lazy, and it all just snowballs.

[7]. Like, you know for a fact that Katie Smith's room is so messy she hasn't even *seen* the floor in years, and her mum never mentions it!

Arguments like this are, sadly, very common, and they all boil down to the same disagreement: when it comes to housework (laundry, cleaning and so on), most teenagers feel they're asked to do too much, while their parents think they don't do nearly enough.

It often ends up with them accusing you of 'treating the house like a hotel', because you expect everyone else to do all the cleaning and picking up after you, like staff in a hotel.

Only, this fundamental **difference of opinion** doesn't just happen when it comes to doing housework, does it?

IT'S LITERALLY EVERYTHING

Is there a song, or a type of music, or a TV show you love that your parents insist is rubbish? Is there something you really want, even *need*, that they tell you is a waste of money? Is there an issue that really matters to you, or has someone said or done something that really upsets you, but when you tell your parents about it they just shrug? Or worse, *laugh*? What are they, psychopaths? How is it so difficult for them to recognize your point of view, your feelings?

It's not like you're saying anything complicated either. For instance, I know many teenagers whose ambition is to be a famous YouTuber. Their parents, however, laugh at this, or dismiss it outright, stressing the importance of getting a 'proper' job or career.

But a quick google reveals that successful YouTubers are often multimillionaires!
How is that not a 'proper' job?

Your parents might say it's not just about money; it's about doing something worthwhile, or useful.

But I bet, if you ended up a professional footballer or a famous musician, they'd be thrilled. Playing a game with a ball, or making catchy noises for a living – how exactly are these things 'useful' or 'worthwhile'? Sure, they make countless people happy. But so do YouTubers, with their millions of followers. Why is entertaining people only meaningful if it's done on the pitch or on stage, but not on YouTube?

Why are things your parents grew up with 'proper' and important, while the things you're growing up with now are not?

If you're thinking this doesn't make any logical sense, you're right. It doesn't. Why is this, along with so many other things, so hard for parents to grasp?

It's almost as if they have a different sort of brain altogether; one that can't see things the way yours can.

In actual fact, that's *exactly* what's going on.

There *has* been a sudden and radical brain change, one that affects how it works, and alters the established relationship between parent and teenager.

Except it's not your parents' brains that have changed. **It's *yours*.**

So, what's happening?

HOW BRAINS WORK

It all comes down to how the brain learns and remembers things. Every newly learned fact or memory, every bit of information we absorb, means a new connection has been formed in the brain, between two cells known as neurons.

How many neurons in the typical human brain? *Around 100 billion!*[8] This allows your brain to perform many billions of functions, actions and processes. That is why the brain is so complicated and powerful.

Although there are other types of cell in your brain, when anyone talks about brain cells, they usually mean neurons. Neurons (which look a bit like a cross between a tree and a spider) link with other neurons, and pass signals back and forth across the brain. This is how the brain does literally everything.

8. Did you know, if you took every cell that makes up a person's brain and laid them out end to end, that person would be dead? And you'd go to jail. So don't do that.

To make this happen, neurons regularly grow branches and connect to other neurons, and many of these connections, usually called synapses, represent a single bit of information in the brain. Like a letter on a page, or a pixel on a screen.

It's actually way more complicated than this, but the main point is, whenever we learn a new bit of information, a new connection between neurons is formed in the brain.

Now, for the first few years of life, especially from birth to age two, your new, mostly empty brain is hoovering up everything at an incredible rate, forming a ridiculous number of connections.

Some estimates are as high as **a million new connections . . . every second!**

So, you soon end up with *trillions* of connections in your youthful brain. And why not? You're a brand-new person, you've no clue how anything works, so every bit of information you encounter might be useful. Vital, even.

But, eventually, **this leads to problems**.

'STORAGE IS ALMOST FULL'

Imagine you're given the latest-model smartphone, and you're so excited that you download literally every app you come across. Because you can!

It'll be fine at first, but soon all those apps will drain the processing power and clog up the storage, slowing the whole thing down. Even if you need something simple like the calculator, you'll need to flip through thousands of icons across hundreds of screens.

What you'd then do, presumably, is delete all the apps you've never opened, or don't like. Essentially, during your teens, your brain's doing the same thing. A human brain is a hugely demanding organ, and it needs 30 per cent of your body's energy supplies just to *stay alive*. So, anything taking up space and resources for no reason is not good.

So, the teenage brain has a clear-out.
Except it's not apps, it's childhood memories.

Because you're *not* a child any more; you're older, more mature, and your brain is now getting ready for life as an independent adult. All that stuff you picked up during childhood – how much of it are you ever going to *use*? Knowing who your friends are, sure. Knowing that a certain type of food makes you sick, great. How to walk and read and count, obviously keep all that.

But remembering a car ride to the supermarket on a rainy Saturday? Or the name of a teddy bear in a cartoon you watched twice? None of this information is of any use, so the brain just . . . gets rid of it.

Just like apps in a phone, 'more' connections in the brain doesn't mean 'better'.

So, during your teenage years, fundamental processes kick in and useless connections get deleted.

As a result, your teenage brain has far *fewer* connections than it did at age five. And this helps, because now it can operate without all that useless junk data clogging up the works. Basically, your brain is updating to an adult form, changing itself to perform better in a new setting.

However, it's not *exactly* like a technological update. Mainly because, while our devices and software are in the process of updating, we generally *can't use them*.

Unfortunately, the updating process in your brain takes *many* years. It starts at age eleven, and doesn't completely finish until you're in *your mid-twenties*!

However, you have to keep using your brain, **because you can't just go to bed for over a decade**.

On top of that, updating your brain isn't just a matter of clearing away clutter. It's also about making things run better, faster, more efficiently.

Again, all this is *meant* to happen. You've probably been told repeatedly (or noticed yourself) that your body changes radically during your teenage years (gaining hair and height and other unexpected things). Why *wouldn't* your brain do the same?

But while your body is *gaining* many new things (for better or worse), your **brain's actually *losing* bits**.

Don't panic – this is a good thing. Like how getting a haircut is a good thing. Except the hair is on the *inside* of your skull.

Actually, that sounds horrifying. I'm going to have to explain this better.

YOUR BRAIN AS A NATIVITY PLAY

Think of all the parts and processes in your brain as the cast and crew in the school nativity play. Everyone is given a specific role and lines, and they learn these quickly and perform them well (or at least acceptably).

But here's the problem: there's no time for rehearsals! Everyone's just shoved on to the stage at the same time, in front of an audience, and left to figure out what to do themselves.

So, you've got the shepherds fighting with the wise men over who stands where, Mary holding the baby upside down, and kids in sheep costumes wandering everywhere, some of them mooing.

This is basically what a child's brain is like up until the age of about eleven.[9]

9. This explains so much about primary school . . .

Then you hit your teens. If your childhood brain is a chaotic performance, your teenage brain is when the teacher in charge arrives, and starts yelling instructions like:

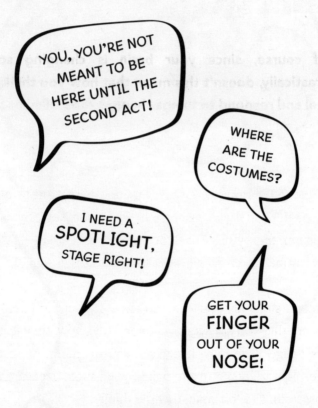

That's what's happening to your maturing teenage brain: all the individual elements know *how* to do their jobs, but they're now being organized and arranged to give as slick, as *efficient* a performance as possible.

THINGS FEEL DIFFERENT

Of course, since your brain is changing so drastically, doesn't this mean that how you think, feel and respond to things changes too? Of course. How could it not?

For example, while your brain ditches useless childhood memories, it obviously doesn't get rid of *all* of them. You'll still remember a beloved soft toy or cartoon, or anything else you enjoyed as a small child. You probably remember such things yourself, right?

Except, suddenly you . . . aren't bothered about them? It's not that you *hate* your childhood toys now; they just don't trigger the same feelings in you any more. Almost overnight they go from being your most treasured possessions to 'oh yeah, that old thing'.

This happens to every teenager. There are certain parts of your brain that control reward and pleasure; anything that makes you feel nice and happy (like your favourite childhood thing). These parts of the brain create that feeling like a bulb creating light.[10] Reward-producing brain pathways are very important, and influence a lot of what we do, say and think. They determine whether we *like*, or enjoy, something.

And how much of your behaviour is geared towards doing or getting things you like? Quite a lot. **That's true for everyone.**

We'll come back to this again and again, but it's important to realize that, very often, when you find yourself making certain choices, it's not because you're lazy or faulty, but because of how your brain

10. As we'll see in later chapters, it's really hard to fight against the things that set off pleasure in our brains.

has evolved: certain things feel pleasurable and some things just don't.

The thing is, these parts are updated like everything else in the brain. And once they've changed, the things that used to trigger them so strongly aren't as good at doing that any more.

Your newly matured brain pleasure system sees your childhood favourites as still recognizably things you like and remember fondly; however, you now need richer, more advanced things to *really* trigger a satisfying response.

BORING!

BORING!

Many parents get exasperated when their teenage child says that things they always used to like are now 'boring'. But those things *are* boring now.

BORING!

As your brain matures, your perceptions, your motivations, your emotions and your behaviour – they all change.

And it's not just *things* you perceive and react to differently; it's people and your relationships with them too. Most obviously, your parents. Whether you intended it or not (and you almost certainly didn't), your attitude and behaviour towards your parents *has* changed as you've grown and matured. And your parents will definitely have noticed this, and will probably have changed in their response to you.

What's this got to do with where you put the wet towels? Trust me, we're getting to that.

DIFFERENT PARTS OF YOUR BRAIN MATURE AT DIFFERENT TIMES

Ideally, given how profoundly this brain-maturing process affects you, it would happen in a logical manner. But, of course, it doesn't.

The human brain didn't just pop into existence as it is now; it evolved over millions of years. It has lots of different parts that do different things, and the more sophisticated human parts – those responsible for things like thinking, imagination and language – evolved more recently.[11]

Remember, all other species have brains too, and they get along just fine with the basic software package.

11. When I say recently, I mean 2 to 3 million years ago, which is like 'last week' in evolutionary terms.

Emotions, instinct, movement and other essentials – that's all that's needed if you just want to **survive and endure**.

Luckily for us, the human brain went beyond that, and evolved all our shiny new complex abilities. However, the more primitive parts are *still there*. We've changed a lot as a species, but we've never needed to stop breathing or moving, so the parts of the brain responsible for these are still going strong. It's like a modern high-tech house connected to a sewer system built in the nineteenth century: the advanced and the ancient, combined to form a working whole.

Now, here's where it gets especially annoying, for both you *and* your parents.

YOUR BRAIN VS PARENT BRAIN

As we've established, your brain is changing.
Right down at cellular level. Meanwhile your parents'
brains . . . aren't. Their brains *were* doing this, because
they already went through this process when they were
your age. But it's not happening to them any more.

However, it *is* for you. And, as you can imagine, this
results in a lot of incompatibility, leading to arguments
and disputes.

STROPPY!

GRUMPY!

Teenagers are often said to
be prone to emotional outbursts.
Adults (many of whom are parents) tend to use
words like 'stroppy', 'moody', 'grumpy', 'hysterical',
'belligerent' and so on to describe the overly emotional
behaviour shown by teenagers.[12] So, what's going on?

---

12. Yes, the same people who declare World War Three if they find a wet towel on
the floor. And if you spend ten seconds watching any modern news report you'll find
that adults can be pretty emotional too.

Evidence shows that teenagers really *do* struggle to keep a lid on their emotions, and experience them more intensely than adults. True, plenty of adults struggle to control their emotions as well, but for teenagers it's a lot harder.

Going back to the argument about the wet towel, we've talked about how your parents overreact to something that's no big deal. But, if it really isn't, why *don't* you do it? Your parents aren't telling you to sleep on the street or give them a kidney, it's just a bit of helping around the house. Surely that's also no big deal?

And yet, for you, I bet *it feels like it is*. Think back to your own actions from a little while ago, and you'll probably realize that your emotional response to a minor request/instruction is often excessive.

The reasons arguments get so intense is down to another **quirk of your brain**.

THE EMOTIONAL BRAIN

The general set-up in your brain is: those parts that process emotions, instincts and impulses are overseen by the more logical, rational parts of the brain. These parts don't have total control over your emotions – it's more a case of keeping them in check, so they don't cause too much disruption, like a human pulling on the lead of an excited dog to stop it jumping up at strangers and slobbering on their faces.

However, a problem occurs during your teen years. More basic parts of the brain, like those that produce emotions, don't take long to mature, so they reach peak performance early on in the process.

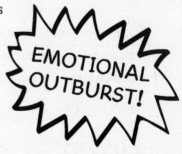

EMOTIONAL OUTBURST!

Meanwhile, more sophisticated areas, like the rational parts that keep our emotions in check, take a lot longer; they're the parts that are still maturing well into your twenties.

It makes sense, really. If you had to build an abacus and a laptop, which would take longer?

More complicated jobs need more time to complete.
That's just a fact.

But this means that, during your teen years, your brain's ability to override emotions isn't fully formed, while your emotions are *as strong as they've ever been*!

YOUR BRAIN AS A SUPPLY TEACHER

Have you ever been taught by a new, inexperienced teacher? Maybe a supply teacher? In many schools, these teachers struggle to keep control of a class; they don't know who's who, how the lessons go, which students are troublemakers, all that.

And we all know who's going to take advantage, playing up and disrupting the lessons because they know more about how things work. It's the troublemakers. The teacher is *technically* in charge, and *can* gain control of the class, but it's much more of a struggle.

In this example, the classroom is your teenage brain, the new teacher is the logical processes (the 'self-control'), the disruptive students are your emotions. That's why teenagers tend to show more emotion than adults: making the logical parts of a teenage brain keep the emotions under control requires way more effort and focus than it ideally should.

Those parts of your brain that produce reward and pleasure respond more readily to things that will be enjoyable *now* than to things that *might* be rewarding at some point down the line, like studying and exams. This can mean that you regularly do things like stay out late with your mates, because that's more fun *now* than avoiding a blazing row with your parents would be *later*.

And coming and going whenever you please, regardless of your parents' wishes? That's another thing that leads to accusations that you 'treat the house like a hotel'.

When it comes to controlling emotions and impulses, because of the way your teenage brain works, it's both more difficult for you to *do* that, and more difficult for you to *want* to.

It's a
double
whammy.

Unfortunately, this *isn't* the case for your parents; it *was* when they were younger, but their brains were done updating ages ago. And this is where disagreements can arise.

For instance, if you feel strongly about something (like wanting to be a YouTuber) and your parents don't, at all, of *course* you're not going to see eye to eye.

But it's often not that your parents *don't* feel the same way; it's more that they *can't*. Or at least not as intensely, which results in similar arguments. They can *understand* and *appreciate* that you feel as strongly as you do, but their own emotional responses to whatever the matter is will be genuinely different.

Your parents may get that you're upset and angry about being asked to pick up a towel, but they can't see *why* you are. **They don't have the same emotional responses to things as you do.**

All this makes it seem like teenagers get quite a raw deal; you need to work ten times as hard to keep your emotions and impulses in check, while your cool, calm parents can be totally rational and logical whenever they like! This surely means that you are *more* likely to argue, *more* likely to get angry, but *less* likely to be right? Your parents can assume you're just 'being emotional'.

And they'll be right?

Thanks a lot, nature. **Really appreciate it.**

But before writing off your brain as a big old mess, don't despair, because evidence shows that this is a very useful, even *vital* set-up.

The sad fact is, teenagers are often mocked and criticized by adults (yes, parents included) for being emotional or dramatic, but this attitude is both unfair and hugely unhelpful. If anything, you should be praised for keeping your emotions under control as much as you do, given how your brain now works.

In truth, you should *never* feel bad about having an emotional reaction. That is *not* a failing on your part. It's actually essential for good mental health and well-being, especially at your age, when your brain is learning *how* to deal with emotions. You can't expect someone to learn maths if you yell at them whenever they open a textbook.

And if you *do* feel emotionally overwhelmed and need to let it out, then . . . have at it. Scream into a pillow, punch a wall, run a mile, spend a few hours slaughtering aliens on your console. Whatever works for you, as long as nobody (including you) gets hurt. Teenagers who do this are being no more *overemotional* than someone trying to stamp out the fire in their kitchen is being *overcautious*.

Overly powerful emotions of the teenage brain aren't just a glitch in the software; they're *meant to be happening*. You're not doing anything wrong: by being emotional and argumentative, you're doing *exactly what nature wants*!

But . . . **why?**

WHAT'S THE POINT?

Well, social species like humans tend to form groups, tribes, packs and so on. Groups provide safety. Strength in numbers. This is particularly true for *family* groups, where vulnerable youngsters are cared for and protected by those most committed to them – parents.

But while safety is often a good thing, always playing it safe leads to a lack of learning and adaptation.

The world is constantly changing to survive and, to survive, you must change with it.

Say you're a species that only eats purple berries, because they're fine and safe. But then purple berries suddenly become infected with a deadly disease. Do you keep eating them and hope for the best? Or are you bold enough to try the yellow ones? If a species is unwilling, or unable, to break out of what they've done before, it can mean extinction.

So, how does a species keep all the benefits of playing it safe while also embracing **change and the unknown**?

Well, what if certain members of the species, especially those in their physical prime and at their most mentally flexible and adventurous, had a strong tendency to seek out the new, and rebel against what they'd always done and typical authority figures (e.g. parents); to meet strangers and experience new things; to boldly go where no one has gone before?

All the stuff you used to find fun and enjoyable is a bit outdated and, with your overhauled brain, it's not just that you're better equipped to deal with change; **you actively embrace it**! **You seek it out.**

Your brain is geared towards asserting independence, seeking out the exciting, throwing off the familiar, exploring the new and rejecting established authority figures. That's how you've *evolved*.

Those very behaviours – rebellion, independence, risk-taking, sensation-seeking and all the other things teenagers are criticized for – are what allowed the human race to explore, adapt and spread our genes far and wide.

Looking at it like this, you could say teenagers are the driving force behind **the success of humanity**.[13]

What this means is that your brain is very flexible, and

13. And what thanks do you get? Not a lot. But forget to put a dish in the sink when you're done with it? Then you'll never hear the end of it.

more open to new ideas and experiences. In important matters like race, sexuality, drugs, gender, gun control, environmentalism, animal rights and more, young people like you are the ones who come to terms with and adapt to the biggest changes while barely missing a step. That's why you rarely hear a teenager complaining about having to use new language to describe a group of people, or when issues like gender or sexuality, or how we eat, get more complicated.

Trying to get your parents to see things from your perspective can sometimes be like trying to play a DVD in a microwave: **you don't get anything useful – you just risk things exploding**.

Millions of years of evolution has produced fundamental differences between adults and teenagers in behaviours, emotions and thinking, stemming from major changes in the very structure of the brain itself.

Doesn't seem so trivial when you look at it like that, does it?

So let's go back to you 'treating your house like a hotel' with all our new brain understanding.

BACK TO THOSE DAMP TOWELS

Are your parents malfunctioning?

First, it's important to recognize that, in your parents' version of events, they're probably right. Treating someone's house like a hotel is not a good thing. I mean, imagine if a strange bloke wandered into your house and started taking food from the fridge and sleeping in the spare room for days on end.

If this happened, your parents should certainly be giving this person an angry telling-off for treating their house like a hotel.[14]

But . . .
you're *not* a stranger.
You're their *child*!

14. They should also probably call the police.

Remember how they used to describe you – it probably makes you a bit queasy now:

PRECIOUS!

PRINCE/ PRINCESS!

PUKE!

DARLING!

APPLE OF MY EYE.

That's the key point. From your perspective, with your parents doing all the necessary jobs to maintain the household, that's just the way *it's always been*. 'The house', as they call it, is *your home*. Who can blame you for treating it as such, when you've been doing that *all your life*? With your parents' blessing! At least, until now.

And this wasn't something you *forced on them*. Many of us over the years, during one of these heated rows with our parents, have yelled, 'I didn't ask to be born!' Maybe you've shouted this yourself? Most parents would laugh or scoff at this, saying you're being 'melodramatic'. But the thing is, it's true. It was your parents who brought you into this world, and made sure you were 100 per cent provided for.

You didn't present them with a big list of never-ending chores the moment you were born. This was an arrangement they set up *themselves*. But now they're not happy with that? Now, suddenly, if you're not doing your own household chores, you're not keeping up your end of the deal.

Except . . . where did **this 'deal' come from**?

It's a totally different arrangement to the one that's been in place your whole childhood. You weren't asked about it. Were you even told that things would be different now?

So, to summarize, here's what happens:

COUNTDOWN TO ARGUMENT

10 **When you're very young, your parents control your whole life, because they *have* to.** They care about you more than anything, and look after you. In turn, you're totally bound to them; they shape your world, they provide nearly every frame of reference your young mind relies on.

9 **But then you hit your teenage years.** Your brain changes gear, and what was once safe and reassuring now seems dull and confining, *including* the relationship you have with your parents. They could be the greatest parents **ever**, but to the teenage brain they'll still go from providers and protectors to controllers and gatekeepers. And your behaviour towards them will change accordingly, often without you even realizing it.

8 **Obviously, this is disconcerting for your parents, and their old**

brains take way longer to adapt to new situations. Especially as they don't see all the stuff going on in your head. They just see you, their *child*, who's not *supposed* to want to do all these new things and like all this new stuff.[15] You're changing things! You're *breaking the contract*.

7 **And there's why your parents suddenly complain so much about you treating the house like a hotel.** The truth is, you have *always* treated the house like a hotel, by assuming your parents will take care of all the housework. Because for your whole life thus far, they *did*!

6 **Your parents used to be OK with this**; their 'payment' was having an engaged and enthusiastic child. They had unquestioned authority over this child, and were involved in every aspect of their life. Because, despite all the work, stress, hassle and complaints, having a child is really rewarding and pleasurable.[16]

15. And we know what they're like with new stuff.
16. Evolution knows what it's doing. That's sort of the whole point.

5 But, if your parents aren't getting the usual benefits from your relationship, there's less motivation for them to supply you with yours. Everything that was taken for granted is now being called into question, even if it's something as seemingly trivial as not picking up a wet towel.

4 But this doesn't mean it's any more enjoyable from your perspective, and most of the time it's certainly not your fault. You're maturing, growing, advancing, and there's nothing to be done about that. The reason why this is so troubling to the teenage brain isn't because your parents are telling you to do something minor; it's because your *parents* are *telling* you to do anything at all, denying you the independence you really want. **Need!**

3 Your parents may often 'lose it' when you don't behave in all the ways they're familiar with and previously enjoyed, but that's not really right or fair, any more than it would be if they insisted on wheeling you around in a pushchair. Sure, it might be distressing for your parents, who don't know how to deal with it and want to maintain the existing relationship with their child. But that doesn't mean they *can* – or that it's right or fair to – take it out on you when the old arrangements no longer apply. And that's why, just when you seem to want to be treated like an adult, they are especially annoyed to find that you don't take responsibility for doing the simple things around the house that an adult does.

2 Sadly, the effect of your parents' fixed brains is that you are accused of being lazy or ungrateful. You might even *believe* this. But it's *not* true. You haven't failed as a person or developed some deep character flaw; it's just that your own brain largely rejects the familiar and the mundane (like doing housework), while for many years your parents have been working hard to provide a safe, comfortable environment for them and their child (often by doing housework).

1 To put it simply, because of the way your brain now operates, teenagers like you genuinely *cannot* care as much about maintaining the house as your parents do. They in turn *cannot* see why you care so much about other things, like hanging out with your friends.

We
have
lift-off!

You might wonder why it's down to *you* to figure out and deal with your parents' issues. Aren't *they* the 'grown-ups' here? But just remember, you're the one with the adaptable and flexible brain: you can better understand this new relationship with its new rules.

It helps to be as patient as you can with parents. It can take the poor things a while to catch up.

TROUBLESHOOTING

THE PROBLEM: **Constant arguments with your parents**, which stem from the fact that they think 'you treat the house like a hotel!'

THE CONSEQUENCES: **Constant, inescapable arguments that can be triggered by very minor things or harmless disagreements.** These arguments can lead to constant stress, impaired mental health and well-being, and a souring of the relationship you have with your parents, which will be crucially important throughout your adult life, even if it doesn't seem like that now.

THE END RESULT: **Your parents feel you ignore what's important to concentrate on things that don't matter.** And you often feel exactly the same about them and are way more likely to have an intense emotional response to disagreements.

THE SOLUTIONS

1 **Avoid getting into arguments with your parents while your emotions are running high.** Try to hold off replying until you feel calmer. It's not that you *shouldn't* respond and just suck it up, but if you can, put off replying for a few minutes. Anything that can help you to be calmer in your approach will stop things escalating.

2 **Just *knowing* what's going on can help on both sides.** Uncertainty often increases stress and anxiety. Try explaining your perspective to your parents when you, and they, are in a good, or at least calm, mood.

3 **Do a deal.** You'll do your own laundry if they get off your back about spending too much time with your friends or not doing your schoolwork.

4 **Try helping around the house without being asked.** The changing dynamic between you and your parents doesn't have to be hostile. Just showing them that you recognize that housework is necessary and that you're willing to do it can diffuse a lot of friction.

It can often feel like every waking moment is spent arguing with your parents but, as we'll find out, it doesn't even stop when you're asleep . . .

CHAPTER 2

'GET UP OR YOU'LL MISS THE BEST PART OF THE DAY!'

>>>**FAULT:** Parents have become obsessed with the amount of sleep the teenager is getting.

DO YOU SLEEP TOO MUCH?

Actually, let's rephrase that: do *your parents say you sleep too much?* Teenagers get accused of this all the time. I know I was at your age.

When you think about it, this is a pretty weird claim. Accusing you of not doing enough housework is one thing – technically you *could* be doing more housework, it's just that you deliberately *don't*, or *won't*. The key word is *deliberate*: your parents believe you've made a *choice* not to help around the house.

Obviously, they feel this choice is the wrong one.

But . . .
sleeping **too much**?
How is *that* a choice?

Who closes their eyes in bed and thinks, *I'm going to sleep for eleven hours. That'll show 'em!* When we're sleeping, we're . . . you know . . . *asleep!* We don't get to make any decisions about the matter.

Have you ever been in the middle of an intense dream, where you're late for school and you haven't done your homework and you're only wearing a really short T-shirt[17] and suddenly thought, *Ah, it's 7:30 – time to wake up.*

No, of course not. You wake up when you finish sleeping, or when something, like an alarm clock, *wakes* you up. Either way, you don't decide when to wake up. Nobody does.

But try telling parents that! You might have woken up late morning, or even early afternoon, prised yourself out of bed and trudged downstairs, still dazed and confused about who you are and what foot goes where, only to be greeted by cries of:

WELL, LOOK WHO DECIDED TO SHOW UP!

MY GOD, IT'S ALIVE!

YOU'VE MISSED THE BEST PART OF THE DAY!

17. This is a very common dream, apparently.

If this hasn't happened to you yet, it probably will. **Soon.**

It's easy to see the point your parents are making here: you sleep too much. You *could* get up much earlier, doing useful or even enjoyable things, but instead you opt to stay in bed. So, when you *do* finally get up, you're apparently fair game for criticism and mockery.

Of course, your standard-model parent will point out that you wouldn't sleep in so long if you went to bed at a sensible time. But the typical teenager doesn't go to bed at a sensible time.

Do you?
Be honest with yourself.

The thing is, though, you don't decide when you're tired any more than you decide how long to sleep for. You'd think parents would know this, given how often they complain about being exhausted; if you can just decide when to be tired, why can't they just decide *not* to be? Simple, right?

The point is, you can try to go to sleep at 8 p.m. all you like, but if you're genuinely not tired, you won't be able to. It's like trying to eat a full dinner less than an hour after lunch: very hard to do, and your parents nagging you to clear your plate doesn't make it any easier.

Would your parents really prefer it if you went to bed at the sensible time of 8 or 9 p.m. and just lay there in the dark, staring at the ceiling? For hours on end? **What, exactly, is sensible about that?**

So, teenagers get a hard time from their parents if they sleep too much, and get a hard time if they don't sleep enough.

As a result, teenagers end up quarrelling with their parents over how much they should sleep, and when.

So, what exactly do parents *want*? What is it with these impossible, self-defeating sleep-based demands?

OK, so there's a lot going on here.

Firstly, let's look at *why* a typical parent should be so obsessed with their teenager's sleep. When you're asleep, you're not *doing anything*. If parents are so exasperated when you cause them extra housework, or watch online videos, or go out and see friends, they should be *glad* when you sleep more. It's less hassle for them.

But no, not content with overseeing every other aspect of your daily life, they need **to butt in when you're *unconscious* too**.

This may be how it seems to you, but it is actually a pretty unfair conclusion.

'WHY ARE THEY OBSESSED WITH MY SLEEP?'

In defence of parents everywhere, while their apparent fixation with your sleeping habits may seem intrusive and annoying, you should know that the sleep of their child (you) has been a **huge** part of their lives since day one. In fact, as soon as there's a newborn baby to deal with, sleep becomes one of the core themes of a parent's existence.

Or, more accurately, the *lack* of sleep.

Babies may be tiny, but they're growing at a frightening rate. That's why they need feeding every few hours, even through the night. Obviously, it's their parents who feed them. And, obviously, they must be awake to do it.

Bottom line: when an adult becomes a parent, they go from having sufficient sleep to *never* having enough.

And what little they do have is disrupted and broken, because they're constantly tending to a tiny human who can't grasp reason or logic but does yell a lot. Since a newborn turns life upside down, parents focus on things like how the baby is eating, sleeping and filling their nappies in order to feel more in control.[18]

However, even when a baby becomes a child and starts doing the much more helpful 'solid, unbroken night's sleep' thing, parents are still significantly affected by their child's sleep patterns.

When you have a child, making sure that child is cared for is more important than anything else. So, housework, finances, paperwork, car maintenance and so on must be squeezed in whenever the child *doesn't* need direct care and attention.

---

18. In fact, it's highly likely that when you were small, your parents were keeping track of when you went to the toilet and what the consistency of your poo was. You're lucky it's only your sleep they're concerned about now.

For many parents, that's when their child is asleep. *That's* the time they have to do other non-child-related jobs, before sleeping themselves.

Or, in fairness, maybe parents just need the time to unwind and relax? Looking after children, no matter how much you love them, is draining, especially as the average child has about eleven thousand times as much energy as the average parent (or so it seems to us adults). Either way, the later a child stays up, the *less* time a parent has for doing other important things, including recovering from an exhausting day.

On top of this, children have to go to school. And school starts in the morning. So, possibly before they have to go to work themselves, a parent must get the children *ready* for school, maybe even take them there.

Logically, the child needs to be awake early enough so that there's time to get them ready for school. This becomes considerably harder if the child *doesn't get enough sleep*. And, with some children, this happens all the time.[19]

Being a parent usually means many years of keeping track of when, and how, your child sleeps.

Having said that, eventually, with a bit of luck, a workable routine is established, whereby the sleep patterns of both parent and child fit in with daily schedules and demands, and everything chugs along nicely.

But then you hit your teens, and those established sleep patterns are thrown **totally out of whack**.

19. If my daughter is reading this, then yes, I absolutely am referring to you.

Teenagers, as we know, typically go to bed late, sleep for a long time, and wake up late. More than that, the build-up to sleep – the 'bedtime routine' – which was once quiet and intimate, is now a subject of constant argument and tension. Once, you could only get to sleep after your parents had read you a story; now, you seem to be doing everything you can to avoid being conscious when they are.

This will surely be a jarring shift for your parents, and we now know they're not the best at handling that.

But, in defence of your parents, you've probably noticed that your sleep patterns have changed a fair bit since you were a kid. You *do* tend to stay up a lot later than you used to, and you tend to sleep in more. Doesn't this mean that your parents are *right* to be concerned? Doesn't it mean that you have a problem?

HOW MUCH SLEEP IS THE RIGHT AMOUNT?

Let's clear this up right away. No, you do *not* have a problem.

Another consequence of being a teenager, and of all the changes it brings about in you, is that it plays merry havoc with your sleeping requirements. In truth, if you analyse what's happening inside the teenage brain when it comes to sleep, it's actually parents who are being unreasonable.

They may not *know* it, but they are.

For instance, if someone's just woken up and they're groggy and confused, the last thing you should do is bombard them with criticism and mockery. They're in a very delicate state, and it may put them on a downer for the rest of the day.

Parents who do this to their teenage children are usually the same ones who will later demand to know why they're always grumpy or moody. It's like tying someone's shoelaces together, then calling them clumsy because they keep falling over.

I'M NOT TRYING TO UPSET YOU, BUT YOU SLEEP TOO MUCH.

Your parents believe that sleeping too much is not helpful or healthy, so to highlight and discourage it is no bad thing, right?

IF YOU WANT TO BE TREATED LIKE AN ADULT...

Well, adults constantly poke fun at each other. And you know what else we do? Get up on time!

You can see how something as simple and familiar as sleeping can cause friction between parent and teenager. Is there any way to reconcile this?

Possibly.

You can see now why your parents have objections to your new, weird sleeping behaviour.

But here's why these objections are wrong.

You may be sleeping at different *times* to your parents, which is something they're not used to, but you're genuinely not sleeping too much. Far from it. Because teenagers need *more sleep*. That's a fact. So, what was enough sleep for you as a child, suddenly . . . isn't.

Sadly, most parents don't know this, so, probably with the best of intentions, they keep waking you up early, bursting into your room at 8 a.m., throwing back the curtains and (loudly) saying, 'Up and at 'em! It's a beautiful day,' or something equally annoying.

They may think they're helping, but in fact it's the opposite. They're *depriving* you of sleep. Sleep that you need.

And this leads to problems, some of which can be very serious.

To understand all the issues your parents have with your sleep, we need to look at sleep itself.

Namely, why do we do it? **What's it *for*?**

WHY DO WE SLEEP?

Sleep seems to have multiple purposes. We scientists haven't quite figured out what all of them are yet. But sleep is important. Vitally so. We know that much.

Now, many assume that sleep is all about rest. You spend a day doing stuff, you sleep to rest and recuperate, you start again the next day, right? This is partly why sleeping late is so frowned upon. If sleep is purely about resting and relaxing, then yeah, sleeping for longer than you should appears lazy and indulgent.

Here's the thing, though: even if sleep *were* just about resting, that's still *incredibly important* for your body.

Sleep allows our bodies essential downtime, to build up all the energy stores depleted during the day and to carry out maintenance and repairs. This stuff isn't trivial: sleep-deprived people typically experience slower metabolisms, gain weight and even take longer to heal from wounds.

So, yes, sleep does provide crucial rest for our bodies.

Sleep and the brain have a rather different relationship, though. It's one that's often misunderstood.

If you compare a sleeping brain to a waking one, there's not much difference in levels of activity. The sleeping brain is working *just as hard* as one that's awake. But working on different things.

Think of it like that old riddle: 'What's heavier, a ton of bricks or a ton of feathers?' The answer, obviously, is neither; they both weigh a ton. The clue's in the question.

But while they may *weigh* the same, a ton of bricks would certainly *look* different to a ton of feathers (e.g. one could fit into a van, the other would need a warehouse). That's kind of what's happening in the brain: **the same amount of activity while awake or asleep, but expressed very differently.**

So, as far as the brain is concerned, sleeping isn't 'rest' time (although some bits are a lot quieter than when we're awake). It's more about doing *different kinds* of work; work that is harder or impossible to do when you're awake and everything's in use.

One crucial process happening in the brain during sleep is **clearing away waste**.

Remember, your brain is made up of billions of cells performing trillions of tasks every second. *All* these involve elaborate chemical reactions, where less useful substances are converted into useful ones.

But, as with most processes, there are always unusable by-products. (If you burn wood you get ash.) Your brain generates a load of chemical rubbish, so, when we're asleep, it's clearing out the trash.

While this happens while we're awake too, it's not enough. You can wash your hands or brush yourself down countless times in a day, but you're still going to need a shower eventually, right? Grime builds up faster than you can get rid of it, so you regularly need to stop, strip off and give yourself a serious scrubbing.

Imagine if you didn't shower for a month. Whatever your standards of hygiene, you'd start to look and smell . . . not great.[20] And the risk of getting sick, with all that dirt and grime clinging to you, increases.

In many ways, not sleeping for the brain is like not showering for the body; if you don't clear out the gunk regularly, it causes problems and it's harder to get anything done.

But there is another crucial process that occurs in the brain during sleep: sorting out the results of learning and memory.

We know now that every new memory or bit of information the brain takes in means a new connection between brain cells is formed. But that's not the end of the story. All these new connections need to be arranged, sorted and processed.

---

20. Again, I am definitely not saying you stink.

MEET KEVIN THE BUDGIE

Imagine you're told that your friend's got a new budgie, and named it, let's say, Kevin. That's new information, a new memory. But it doesn't just sit in your head, isolated. You don't think to yourself, *I am aware of the existence of a budgie named Kevin*, and that's it.

No, this new knowledge, this new memory, is connected to *existing* knowledge and memories. Like the memories concerning your friend – you'll remember that they have a budgie now, and that it'll be there when you visit their house.

It's also connected to your memories of budgies and other birds, so you know what it is, what it'll look like.

You've never seen it, but you still *know* it won't have tentacles, or be wearing clown shoes. Because the new memory has been properly sorted.

You might also think, *Kevin is a weird name for a budgie.*

This is because the new memory has been connected to your memories of every other Kevin you know, and they're all human males, so this new one stands out. But it wouldn't stand out if it wasn't properly processed and connected to all the other ones for comparison.

You can download to your smartphone all the apps and files you like, but if they're not part of the operating system, they're meaningless. It's just useless noise, taking up space. And the same goes for your brain, but with memories.

THE BRAIN LIBRARY

Think of it as a library, one that's the size of a city.
Every day, as soon as it opens, books are coming in. Tens of thousands of them, with existing books being returned, and new ones delivered by the truckload.

They all need to be sorted, otherwise no one can find them when they need them. So the army of staff at this library do their best, but they can never keep up with this huge, constant flow. However, once the library closes in the evening, and the trucks full of books stop arriving, *that's* when they can deal with them all.

At night, thousands of people carry trolleys of books to the right shelves, or several copies to different shelves, sliding them in alongside older books in the same category, or transferring old books to new shelves because their labelling's been changed.

There are hundreds of carpenters and labourers too, frantically putting up new bookshelves, taking down old, empty ones, and on and on.

This library is your brain. The books are all the things you learn and experience and remember every day. And when's the library closed? That's when you're asleep. It might look dark and quiet from the outside, but there's a frantic amount of sorting and processing of information happening within.

DREAM ON

And finally there's the matter of dreaming.

This is a tricky one. Sleep isn't a simple process. There are several stages, and dreams occur during the stage known as REM (rapid eye movement) sleep. It's called this because when it happens, our eyes twitch around frantically behind our eyelids. The brain itself suddenly bursts into life during this stage; brain activity during REM sleep looks pretty much the same as when we're awake. Our heart rate and respiration can go doolally too.

Why? Well, we don't know. Exactly why REM sleep happens as it does and why dreams occur – the jury's still out on that. But many (me included) think that it's another aspect of brain upkeep that goes on while we sleep. It's one thing to organize and tweak all these brain connections, but the best way to confirm that they all still work is to activate them. Turn them on, see if they work.

That could be what's happening when we dream. Countless new and old connections, many of which are memories and experiences, are being switched on briefly, to make sure they're working.

Of course, when a memory in the brain is activated, **we relive it, we experience it**.

And if you were to trigger multiple different memories at random, out of all the ones present in your brain, it would create a pretty weird experience – a chain of events with no logic, no coherence, no rules and no obvious pattern. But, as it's made up of memories from inside your own head, there's nothing unfamiliar happening, so it would *still seem reasonable* to you at the time, no matter how bizarre it appears in hindsight.

That sounds like a dream, right?

WE
NEED
SLEEP

The point is, sufficient sleep is *crucial* for a fully functional brain. Our brains are high-performance machines and they need a lot of upkeep. Sleep is when this happens.

Sure, you can *get by* on reduced sleep, but you'll be *compromised*. Without enough sleep, the books aren't being sorted, the rubbish is piling up, which makes day-to-day running more difficult.

And if lack of sleep persists, things get worse. Sleep deprivation is linked to chaotic mood swings and (even more) unstable emotions, leaving you seriously irritable, even prone to disorders like depression (depression and disrupted sleep patterns go hand in hand). Sleep deprivation also makes it harder for you to learn and remember new things, because new information isn't being processed properly. It also makes it much harder to think straight or focus.

That's why insomnia (a serious inability to sleep) is so awful, and why, if you meet someone who's having trouble sleeping, they're usually confused, irritable, absent-minded, even scruffy and unkempt, because making yourself presentable requires focus and coordination, something you lack when you're severely tired.

Now, here's a key point – everything we've just discussed, that's what happens during sleep *in an ordinary adult brain*. That's all just to keep the average person working normally.

But your teenage brain has even more to deal with, and this alters **your sleeping needs and behaviours**.

Unfortunately, most parents (and adults in general) don't know this, so they give you grief about your sleeping habits.

In many ways, this is very unfair. Needing different amounts of sleep at different stages of your life is not exactly an unfamiliar idea. Babies sleep all the time, and old Grandpa Ted is forever nodding off in the armchair when he visits. Do your parents poke babies awake and tell them they're missing the day? Does Grandpa get yelled at and called bone idle? Probably not.

Your parents seem to be fine about indulging other people's sleep requirements. Why not yours?

It's probably to do with the fact that yours are so different to what they're used to. And we know they struggle with that.

FALLING ASLEEP

First, there's the fact that you go to bed too late, by your parents' standards. Even if true, it's still not a deliberate choice; you're not forcing yourself to stay awake just to be annoying. At least, that's not why it starts.

Falling asleep is controlled by many things: activity levels in particular regions in the brain, body temperature, hormones, even genes. These all combine to create your circadian rhythm, also known as your body clock, which decides when it's time to be awake, and when to sleep.

One key aspect of your internal clock is a hormone called melatonin.[21] A part of the brain called the pineal gland starts pumping out melatonin when it's dark outside (it's connected to your eyes so it responds to light levels). When your brain detects a lot of melatonin

---

21. Hormones are chemical messengers. They're substances released into the bloodstream that tell your body, or specific parts of it, to do certain things or bring about specific changes. Your adolescent body is awash with hormones, which is why it keeps doing weird, annoying things.

sloshing around your body, it goes, 'Ah, sleepy time,' and you start to *feel* tired, and gradually wind down to the point where you can sleep.

Studies show that, for most adults, melatonin levels go up at around 10 p.m.

However, for teenagers?
It's 1 a.m.!

That's why it's a problem when your parents tell you to be in bed at a 'reasonable hour': what's reasonable to them *isn't* for you and your body clock. Try telling your parents they have to be in bed by 7 p.m. They'd probably laugh in your face. But that's pretty much what they're saying to you.

Your internal clock is out of alignment with your parents'. So, most parents try to get you to sync with theirs. But it's like trying to get a computer to connect to a printer that isn't turned on; no matter how much you yell, it's not going to happen.

However, your body clock *is* flexible. If you go on holiday to a different time zone, your sleep patterns probably clicked in to local time after a day or two. So, why's it so difficult for you to conform to the sleep routine of *your own home*?

Once again, the internal workings of your teenage body are to blame.

Sleep is controlled by hormones, but when you're a teenager, your body is *flooded with hormones!* So, other hormone-regulated processes, like *sleep*, get messed up as a result.

We've seen that sleep is when the brain takes the rubbish out. Well, sleep during your teenage years is like taking the rubbish out during a thunderstorm. Heavy rain, deafening noise, powerful winds all make things more difficult. It *can* be done, but you often end up upside down in a hedge with the bin bags in the next street.

That's one theory anyway. Another theory is that teenagers' weird sleep patterns are self-imposed.

Because most teenagers *like* to stay up late.

It's understandable. Your day consists of being told what to do and where to go, both at school and at home. Night-time, when everyone else is asleep, is when *you* get to decide what to do. So, sure, you're going to make the most of it, whether you're hanging out with your friends or just doing stuff in your room.

Your parents know the value of having some time to themselves in the evening, so why wouldn't this be true of you?

We can *override* our body clock, if necessary. Countless people push through fatigue and exhaustion if they're doing something important, like driving long distances. And if you keep hitting your brain with intense stimulation – playing video games or other entertainment, or chemically through caffeine and energy drinks – then you can deliberately delay sleep.

However, the *need* for sleep never goes away; your brain and body are still racking up exhaustion, and that's a debt that has to be paid at some point, so you *will* go to sleep eventually. And you'll go *hard*.

Do this often enough – stay up late for weeks on end chatting on social media or playing video games – and your flexible teenage brain will adapt to this new arrangement, and your body clock will adjust.

It's actually a bit of a chicken-and-egg thing here. Do you have a weird body clock because you keep staying up late? Or do you keep staying up late because your body clock has gone weird?

Personally, I think it's the second. And here's why . . .

Teenagers' late hours are often blamed on things like games consoles, smartphones, social media, Wi-Fi and energy drinks. But teenagers were staying up late long before these things were even invented.

I bet your parents, if pushed, will remember times when they stayed up past midnight listening to albums, or sneaking out to parties and returning when everyone else was asleep. And now they give you hassle about the same things?

Hypocrites!

In any case, the fact that it's been happening for generations suggests some underlying cause, rather than simple self-indulgence, despite what many parents (and countless adults in the media) seem to think.

However, staying up late wouldn't be such an issue if you needed the normal amount of sleep, just at different times. But no, you need a lot *more* sleep compared to adults or primary-school children. A typical adult needs seven or eight hours' sleep a night, but teenagers like you could really do with nine or ten, possibly more.

WAKING UP

This brings us to the other issue: teenagers sleeping too late and 'missing' the day. But there are very good reasons why you sleep in, and they have nothing to do with laziness.

Remember, your teenage brain is undergoing major overhauls. So, on top of the usual essential processes that happen while we're asleep, there's all these new changes and developments to deal with and process.

Using that 'brain is a massive library' analogy, it's not just book deliveries that need to be sorted out now. The whole library is being redesigned and reorganized. There's even more work to do behind the scenes, so the library is going to have to stay closed for longer, just to get things done.

To bring it back to the real world, your brain now has a lot more to do while you're asleep. So, logically, you *need more sleep*!

Parents are generally not aware of this, so they will try to impose a more typical sleeping pattern on you. In fairness, their parents probably did the same to them, and your grandparents' parents did the same to them.

Why has this parenting behaviour persisted for so long when it's so unhelpful and even harmful? Maybe the argument is that it works? After all, if you're pressured to get up and start doing stuff early in the morning, you *can* do it. You'll be unhappy and grump and yawn a lot, but you can stay awake. So, you clearly don't *need* so much sleep, right?

This approach is like forcing someone with a horrible cold to leave the house and go to work. Just because they can just push through it *doesn't mean they're not ill*!

And it costs them. They can't do their job as well as they should, and they could even pass on the cold to anyone they meet. Sure, tiredness can't be passed on like a bug, but it's a lot harder to do your job right when you haven't had enough sleep. And when others depend on you (e.g. you're a doctor), your lack of sleep poses a real risk to innocent people.

This is pretty much what your parents are doing when they keep interfering with your sleep patterns. They're making you go to work when you're ill. The fact that you *can* be made to wake up doesn't mean you *should* be.

You *can* technically train a chimp to drive a forklift truck. But, you know, *don't*!

WELL, AT LEAST HE'S NOT ASLEEP

However, if lack of sleep causes such problems, and teenagers' body clocks have been disrupted by well-meaning parents for so many decades, someone would surely have *noticed* by now? Fair point. But think of the classic (and insulting) stereotypes of teenagers that adults love to throw around:

But do you know who all those things describe?

People who are
deprived of sleep!

Could it be that *all* the easily mocked characteristics of teenagers result from the fact that parents constantly stop them getting as much sleep as they need?

There's almost certainly more to it than that, but it makes a worrying amount of sense.

And it doesn't stop there, does it? Being denied sleep means, among other things, that you have less energy and are less able to retain information and focus.

Logically, this is the *worst possible* time to make you study for a load of exams – ones which you're told will affect the rest of your life.

But guess what? That's *exactly* what happens! Teenagers like you are put in a situation where your ability to remember facts and focus at school is more important than ever, but at the same time these abilities are constantly being reduced by well-meaning but clueless parents who won't let you get the sleep you need. It's not all their fault. The modern world has made it a rule that you need to get to school by a certain time, and your parents can't change that. They have to get you out of bed so you won't be late.

Just like the 'treating the house like a hotel' disagreement in the previous chapter, a lot of this comes down to a misalignment between your parents' thinking and your own, caused by the different ways in which your brains are working.

Neither you nor your parents think that sleep *isn't* important. You both agree that it's *really* important. **But you just *don't* agree *when* you should do it, and for *how long*.**

Most parents seem to think that sleeping is like eating. Sure, you *need* to eat, but you can eat too much, or you can eat badly, or at least not sensibly, gorging yourself on sugary or fatty foods. This suggests greed, gluttony and poor self-discipline. And it's their responsibility to stop you doing this.

Parents think about sleep in the same way: it's necessary, but overdoing it is unhealthy and indulgent, and it's up to them to stop you compromising your health and developing bad habits.

But, as we've seen, sleeping is *not* like eating. You can't decide to do it more; you don't get to choose when you're tired or not. Sleeping is more like breathing – another vital function, but one that's dictated by what's going on inside you. And sleeping longer when you need more sleep is the *opposite* of unhealthy!

If your parents criticize you for sleeping too much, it's like **criticizing someone who's just run a marathon for breathing too much**.

This would be dismissed as ridiculous.

And yet your parents do it to you all the time.

Nobody knows your parents better than you. You're familiar with the model you've been brought up by. The problems they have with your sleep are usually based on a genuine desire to help, but one built on misunderstanding and/or missing information.

TROUBLESHOOTING

THE PROBLEM: You are sleeping more, and at unusual times. Your parents try to stop you doing this or criticize you when it happens. But this doesn't change anything, so nobody is happy.

THE CONSEQUENCES: On top of the arguments, you're being denied the sleep you genuinely need. This reduces your mental abilities, causing problems with memory, focus, attention, mood, emotions, coordination, energy levels and so much more. And this means that your parents find further reasons to have a go at you.

THE SOLUTIONS: There are steps you can take to adjust your sleep patterns, which would probably get your parents off your back a bit.

1 **Regular exercise can help.** The more tired you are, the more you're willing or able to sleep. So it makes sense to tire yourself out where you can.

2 **A tendency to go to sleep late can often be made worse by the use of devices like phones and tablets.** Blue light from screens has been shown to interfere with the brain's release of melatonin, that key hormone for triggering sleep. Many modern devices these days have a blue light filter option for this reason. If you've got that, use it.

Such devices are stimulating, which overrides the getting-tired-and-falling-asleep mechanism, keeping you awake. It is wise to unplug for an hour or so before you want to sleep, so your brain can cool down.

Put your devices out of reach, if you can. You'll be a lot less tempted to check them if you wake up in the night (meaning you'll struggle to fall asleep again), because the 'can't be bothered' factor should never be underestimated.

3 **Suggest to your parents that you'll try getting to bed and waking earlier on school days**, if they leave you be to catch up at weekends? You have *good reason* to sleep in, after all. Remember, they almost certainly believe they're *helping* you. You don't like it when they criticize you for something you don't mean to do, and the same goes for them. And a bad response to criticism is made even worse if there's a huge helping of guilt thrown in too.

4 **You could stay up late without being nagged about it if you use some of that time to do something useful.** Do more homework or do some housework. You don't enjoy these things of course, but it's usually a lot easier if they're done on your own terms, without someone breathing down your neck.

So we now know the many reasons why you need to get more sleep; for one thing it means you can cope better with school. Although lack of sleep isn't the only issue there . . .

CHAPTER 3

'SCHOOL DAYS ARE THE BEST DAYS OF YOUR LIFE!'

>>>**FAULT:** Parents are obsessed with asking about school but don't understand that this stresses the teenager out.

Imagine if adults were forced to get up early and go somewhere they didn't want to be. Without pay. Shut in rooms for hours at a time, told where to go and when, who to talk to and what about. Forced to study subjects they have no interest in and warned that failing the exam will ruin their life. And all this while surrounded by friends, and at exactly the moment when their brain is putting them under a tremendous pressure to impress.[22] While their body and brain are changing in new and often unsettling ways, filling them with unfamiliar, intense feelings. Most of the things they used to like and enjoy don't have the same effect any more. To top it all off, they feel constantly tired.

Do you think adults would just put up with all that without complaining? Not a chance.

But does any of this sound *familiar*?

It's time to talk about . . .

---

22. The human brain, particularly the teenage brain, often makes us *obsessed* with being accepted and liked by other people. In later chapters, we'll see why, and how this affects so much of your life.

SCHOOL

Picture the familiar scene: you've made it through another school day, with all the pressure, tension and hassle it involved. You finally get home, tired out, and all you want to do is maybe chill for an hour, and just not think or worry about anything for a while.

However, that's when your parents will usually swoop in with all the questions:

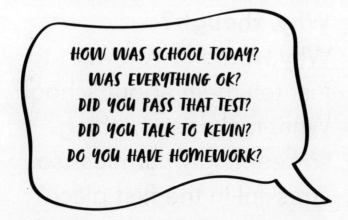

HOW WAS SCHOOL TODAY?
WAS EVERYTHING OK?
DID YOU PASS THAT TEST?
DID YOU TALK TO KEVIN?
DO YOU HAVE HOMEWORK?

The thing is, you've just *been* to school. The last thing you want to do is relive the whole day in exquisite detail. Yet that's what your parents are insisting you do.

So you say it was 'fine' and hope they'll leave it there, or you just admit, 'I don't want to talk about it.' But they assume that you're shutting them out, rejecting them, or that you're in trouble, so will often double down on the intrusive questions. Which makes you feel even more stressed, so you dig your feet in, and yet another argument blows up.

It seems like an impossible situation: you don't want to have to tell your parents about your school day, they insist on hearing all about it, and every possible response leaves nobody happy.

Why, though?
Why *wouldn't* you want to just tell them about school? What makes something so seemingly harmless so stressful in the first place?

At least your parents aren't *responsible* for what happens at school. They aren't even *there*, so they can't be blamed for any unpleasant aspects, right?

While this is true, many parents find ingenious and creative ways to make your school experience yet another source of arguments and stress. Which is a bit much! They are the ones who keep banging on about how important school is (and get upset if you do badly), so you'd think they would want to *avoid* making things harder for you!

But then they're also nagging you for not getting enough sleep, while constantly waking you up early and losing it over wet towels. We've established that many parents aren't logical. And *you're* supposed to be the emotional, irrational one?

In fact, constantly pressuring you to do better at school is guaranteed to make the whole experience worse. Many parents get pretty obsessive over your progress and grades, and urge you to study harder, do your homework early, or take on extra-curricular activities.

It's as if your education is a joint effort, something that affects *both* of you. **Maybe they even think it *is*?**

But the actual work involved falls squarely on *your* shoulders, so your parents' obsession can mean you end up with even *more* work outside school, which increases stress and anxiety.

In fairness, many parents *don't* go on at teenagers to do well at school. But they can still heighten stress just by constantly bringing it up, bombarding you with all the questions.

In these and other ways, your parents can be unhelpful with regard to your school experience. **Why do they do it, and how do you go about dealing with it?**

WHY YOU'RE STRESSED

Again, a lot of it comes down to understanding how your parents' minds (and brains) work, and accepting that they often think very differently to you.

This mismatched thinking can be seen in the way parents make your school-based stress even worse: by denying it exists. Denying that *your stress* exists, I mean, not school.[23]

Maybe you've experienced this? You tell your parents you're stressed about school (or anything really) and, rather than hear you out, they laugh and say something like:

STRESS? YOU DON'T KNOW THE MEANING OF THE WORD!

Amazingly, this response *doesn't* help anyone. Who'd have guessed?

23. Parents never *forget* about school. Even if you hire a hypnotist.

THE MEANING OF STRESS

To clarify, 'stress' is the unpleasant feeling, the negative state of mind, that comes about when you experience something bad (such as bullying, illness or injury, or sitting through lessons you hate) and/or something that makes your life harder than it could, or should, be (housework, a missed bus or train, excessive homework).

It's not 'all in the mind' either. A stressed brain releases chemicals and hormones into your body that cause increased muscle tension, raised blood pressure, altered heart and breathing rates, and more. And your brain becomes more focused on and sensitive to the problem causing this.

So, stress makes you genuinely *feel worse*, **both mentally and physically**.

It's actually something that's *meant* to happen, at least in theory. The feeling we know as stress is the result of your brain's instinctive reaction to fear and danger. When you encounter something that your brain deems to be a threat, or just recognizes as something unpleasant, it begins the process of putting you in a state where you're ready to deal with it, whatever it may be.

It's all pretty unpleasant, but that's *sort of the point*. Think about it: your brain is convinced you're about to experience something bad, even dangerous. It certainly doesn't want you relaxed, happy and comfortable! It wants you on edge, in a position where you're really keen to put a stop to whatever the bad thing is.

Of course, given how life works, whatever the bad thing is, it's often something you have no real say in or control over. But those deep parts of your brain don't realize that. So, they just keep you stressed.[24]

---

24. There. You've read that, so your parents are automatically wrong forever if they say you 'don't know the meaning of stress'. Because now you clearly do.

In any case, you don't *need* to know the meaning in order to *experience* stress. You don't need to understand something in order to use it.

Most parents don't know how a car engine works, **but they still have a driving licence**.

Look at it logically: you say you're feeling stressed, and your parents' response is basically 'No you're not'? That's not how *anything* works! Nobody else gets to decide what's going on *in your head*! If someone says they have a problem, you can't just say they don't, and that's the end of it.

Let's flip it. Imagine using this tactic on your *parents*' complaints:

Would this work? Would your parents say sorry and drop the whole thing? Or would they get fifty thousand times more furious?[25]

25. It would be the second one.

The point is, your parents will struggle to stop adding to your school stress if they don't even *recognize that it exists*.

But *why*? Why can't they, or *won't* they, accept the idea that you're feeling stressed? Because it's *infuriating* that they don't, let's be honest.

The answer to this is hinted at by something else parents (and many other adults) say when you mention you're finding school hard. You ask me, it's one of the most annoying statements known to parent-kind.

'You should be grateful; school days are *the best days of your life*.'

How wonderfully helpful to be told that you should *enjoy* something that causes you such grief because, **apparently, the rest of your life will be *worse*!**

THE BEST DAYS OF YOUR LIFE

Why do parents and other adults say this? Was their school a non-stop party? With water slides? Or a petting zoo?[26]

Of course not. Parents never miss a chance to tell you how much *worse* school was in their day. No calculators or internet; memorizing whole essays and times tables; walking five miles there and back every day.

If your parents are old enough, they might even talk about 'proper' teachers who would (and were allowed to) thrash you senseless with a cane or slipper if they caught you misbehaving.

So yeah, there are parents who insist that school days are the best days of your life while *simultaneously* telling you how horrible their school experience was.

---

26. But not both. That would quickly get very unhygienic.

If that's true, how *incredibly awful* is their life now? And if it's that bad, why on earth would you *listen to their advice* about anything? Because they must have gone severely wrong somewhere.

The thing is, it *isn't* true. Not really. But for many adults it *feels* true, because they were, according to their memory, *less* stressed at school than they are *now*.

This happens because our brains don't usually deal in absolutes or fixed values. As we grow and develop and learn our thinking and understanding and feelings about things – our *perspective* – changes.

As a teenager, you know this better than anyone. It's happened to you a lot, probably very recently.

When you were small, maybe the teacups ride at the fairground was the most exciting ride *ever*? Now, you wouldn't be seen dead on them; you're queuing for the roller coasters. The teacups haven't changed, though. It's still the same ride.

Your parents were once the unquestioned authority, the centre of your existence.

Now, they're those annoying people you're forced to live with who want **to control your life**.

And yet your parents are basically the same people.

As we've seen, we change as we grow, and how we feel about things changes too.

Your parents are a lot older than you. This means they have more *experiences* than you, and experience is a *huge* factor in how you think and react, especially with things like stress.[27]

Think of it like ice cream.

---

27. Being more experienced also tends to make adults think they're smarter. But, as we'll see in a later chapter, they're often wrong about this.

STRESS ICE CREAM

I'm going to assume you like ice cream . . . Loads of people seem to. But imagine you'd only ever had vanilla ice cream. You've not *avoided* other flavours; you genuinely *don't know they exist*. Nobody has ever mentioned them, and you've never been anywhere that sells anything other than vanilla.

You still really *like* ice cream (nothing wrong with vanilla), but your understanding and *experience* of it is rather limited.

And then, one day, you wander into a proper ice-cream parlour. Chocolate, strawberry, hazelnut, cookie dough, salted caramel – they're all there behind the glass.

Obviously, you'd end up indulging in an ice-cream extravaganza. But after that, once you've experienced the full range of ice cream, vanilla isn't quite as pleasurable as it once was.

But again, *vanilla* hasn't changed; *you* have. You've *experienced* more; your knowledge and appreciation of ice cream is now hugely enhanced.

For your parents, stress is like the ice cream, and the ice-cream parlour is adulthood. Except it's not a pleasant experience. It's awful. As if the ice cream caused constant brain freeze.

YOUR PARENTS ARE STRESSED

Your parents probably found school as difficult as you *at the time*, but they've experienced things that are way more stressful since. So, they feel they've a much better idea of what 'real' stress is.

They probably have a point. School is hard, sure, and it asks a great deal of you. But usually it affects *just you*. Exams are bad enough, but imagine how much worse they'd be if failing meant that you *and your three best friends* would be expelled? That's enough pressure to make you sick.

That's life as a parent. They have to work, often at jobs they don't particularly enjoy, to earn money and pay bills. Because if they don't, you'd *all* lose your home. Parenting means providing and caring for a whole family, not just yourself.

There are plenty of brilliant aspects to being a parent; there's just a lot at stake. The highs are higher, but the lows are lower. There are more possible *consequences* to what your parents do, especially if they fail. And they have way more *responsibilities* to fulfil to prevent these consequences.

This is undoubtedly rather stressful.

Ironically, the thing adults can do that results in the most responsibilities, and therefore stress, is have a child, aka *become a parent*.

Suddenly becoming provider and guardian for a tiny helpless human *that you created,* **that's a huge deal**.

Overall, annoying as it may be to admit it, your parents probably do have a much greater experience of stress than you, often *because* they're your parents.

As a result, they can be a bit dismissive of your complaints about school stress. To them, you're the small kid shouting about how vanilla ice cream is the best while they're eating a twelve-flavour sundae.

As you can imagine, the temptation to roll your eyes and scoff, rather than sympathize, is pretty strong.

Imagine how you'd respond if a four-year-old started complaining to you about how stressful nursery is.

HONESTLY, IT'S LIKE,

DO I PLAY WITH THE SANDPIT

OR THE CRAYONS, THE CRAYONS

OR THE SANDPIT?

NIGHTMARE!

However, all this is an explanation. *Not* an *excuse*. Even if you *did* 100 per cent accept that your parents regularly deal with more stressful things, that doesn't change things *for you*. Knowing that someone else might be *more* stressed doesn't make you *less* stressed, any more than knowing someone else had both their legs blown off in an explosion makes your broken ankle feel better.

THE MOST STRESSED PERSON IN THE UNIVERSE

Let's follow the logic of their argument. You can't complain about stress because they've experienced more of it? But surely there's someone out there who's experienced more stress than your parents? So *they* can't complain about stress either?

And there must be someone more stressed than *that* person? And then someone more stressed than *them*? Follow this argument to the end, and it suggests there's one person on Earth who's the most stressed of all. And only *they* can complain about it. Literally everyone else needs to shut up and put up.

But they don't. Because that's *not* how things work. And any parents who think it is, they're just being clueless.

Still, even though it clearly makes things worse, you can sort of see why some parents dismiss the idea that school is stressful.

Of course, not all parents do this. Most of them don't. Even if they do, it doesn't mean they don't *care* about your school life. They may well just want to know how it's going.

It's good that they're interested in what you're up to, right? It's reassuring that they care?

Not necessarily. Because in this case they can often care *too much*.

It's understandable. They've spent many years with 100 per cent involvement in your life, tending to your every need. You've been their responsibility for a *very* long time. But now you spend hours every day out of their sight, in a different place, listening to other people and learning new things. All without them.

We've seen that the adult brain doesn't deal well with change **and this change is a particularly difficult one for parents**.

THEY MISS KNOWING YOU

It's like this: imagine you had a best friend. You've been incredibly close since the moment you could walk. You do everything together, you live next door to each other, you play every game together, regularly share your meals, have sleepovers in each other's houses.

Then suddenly they move away. Their mum gets a new job or something. Not too far away – you still see them regularly, but they go to a different school now, have different friends.

So, when you meet them, would you just ignore the fact that they have this other existence which doesn't include you? Or would you *ask* them about what they get up to, because you really want to know what this person, who is a huge part of your life, gets up to when you're not around?

It would be the second.
Definitely.

For a parent, your child going to school is like that, but five million times more intense.

So, parents often *have to* ask you what you've been up to at school. How could they not? But this causes problems.

Younger children who still see their parents as the very centre of their lives are usually fine with this. They *want* to share and impress their parents.

But for teenagers like you – with your rapidly changing brain giving you a yearning for independence and new experiences, a dislike of authority, and powerful emotional reactions – your parents' constant need to know all about your school progress can be a source of stress and aggro. It doesn't feel like interest; it feels *controlling*. To them it seems like a crazy distance opening up in their relationship with you, between your life and theirs, but to you it feels as if they're constantly looking over your shoulder.

You really need them to back off and let you do your own thing, but being a parent means they never stop giving a damn, even when it's unreasonable.

Their brains
won't let them.

That can be a problem, because much of what happens to you at school . . . isn't great. Bullying, falling out with friends, getting bad marks, detention, embarrassments, it's all there.

But you often feel you know the best way to handle it. You're used to this, it's happening to you, you know how it all came about. Your parents *don't*. And if you *tell* them about it, they could make it worse.

Say you got detention because your friends were messing about in class. You *weren't* messing about, but your teacher knows you're part of the same group, so assumes you were up to no good too. This happens annoyingly often.

No, it isn't *fair*, it's frustrating. But it's also not the end of the world.

Maybe you *do* regularly mess around in this class; you've just not been caught before. Maybe the teacher is a decent one who's just having a bad day. Maybe the teacher is a *bad* one who everyone hates because he does this all the time, so everyone takes your side, meaning you feel included and accepted.

The point is, you can see the big picture, so you can deal with it in ways that work out for the best.

However, your parents *don't* see the big picture. They can't. If you tell them, all they'll hear is: 'I got detention and I shouldn't have.' They might get furious on your behalf, angrily phone the school, loudly demanding to have that teacher sacked, putting all the blame on your friends and insisting that they be punished, and more.

The thing is, *they* don't have to see your teachers and friends the next day. *You* do. So, them dealing with trivial problems with all the calm and restraint of a wild horse in an antique shop is the last thing you need. That causes way more stress for you.

Of course, if you tell them about a (minor) issue that *is* your fault, like a poor test score or a valid detention, they might go nuclear – yelling at *you* and punishing you for 'letting yourself down' and so on. Sure, there's a logic to it: you've done something wrong, and they don't want you to do it again. But honestly, who needs that kind of hassle?

So sure, your parents **can care *too much***.

It's not like you *don't* care, either. Most of the time, you don't really *want* to reject or hurt your parents by refusing to keep them up to speed about school. But it's a very big ask, given all that's going on. So, you're stuck in a lose-lose situation: disappoint them, or pile more stress on yourself. And it's often easier to disappoint them, because there's less chance of a huge overreaction that way. And you have a teenage brain to deal with, one desperate for new experiences rather than recounting stuff you've already dealt with once today!

WHAT ELSE IS GOING ON?

And before you feel guilty about not communicating with your concerned, doting parents, there's a decent chance *they're* not being entirely selfless here.

Earlier, I joked about the idea that your education is a joint effort between you and your parents, but that's *exactly* how many parents see it. Even if they don't realize it.

Most parents want to be considered a *good* parent. And one important way people determine this is by *how well your child is doing at school*. Your parents raised you after all; your behaviour, abilities and intelligence are, according to many, the direct result of the parenting you received. So, any school failings on *your* part can suggest that *your parents* were . . . less than ideal.

So, if you do badly at school, it *does* reflect on your parents. It's not fair, for either of you, but that's just how it is.

No parent wants to hear from the neighbours about how their darling Tammy gets straight As, and spends all her free time embroidering complex equations on to socks for three-legged guide dogs, when their own child has been suspended for selling cigarettes to the eight-year-olds behind the bike sheds.

This would be humiliating for your parents, so they may react badly to anything that suggests you're not doing the best you can at school.

And before you get too angry about this, how many times have you got mad at them for embarrassing you in front of your friends? Imagine that best friend who's moved away again. What if you found out they were doing and saying stuff that made you look bad. You probably wouldn't like it.

Why *wouldn't* the same be true about you and your parents?

That's the thing about such close family bonds: **you affect each other's lives all the time, whether you want to or not.**

Anyway, all this adds up to your parents' constant questions about your school. But it's very common for teenagers to resist telling them about it. This leads to disagreement, more stress, friction and arguments.

MUM, DAD, STOP DOING THAT. YOU'RE *SO* EMBARRASSING!

In fairness, if your parents dismiss the very notion of you being stressed at school, why *would* you share your issues with them? But even if they're genuinely interested and concerned with your school experience, this can still cause problems.

There are several things going on in your head here, none of which your parents will be aware of. You're misaligned, yet again.

Firstly, remember that you're experiencing emotions at a much higher intensity than them. Your parents' emotions are like having the car radio on. Yours are like standing right by the speakers at a loud gig.

Emotions are a big part of memory. The way our brains work, the more emotional an experience is, the better we remember it.

The downside of this is, whenever we remember an emotional memory, we end up *re-experiencing* those emotions. You may 'see' the events that occurred in your head while remembering them, but you're also feeling the same feelings you had.

Ever felt sad when thinking about a family tragedy, or seriously angry when remembering something really unfair? Then you know what I'm talking about.

School can be a particularly intense and emotional experience. You've no choice about being there, you're under constant pressure to perform, and you're surrounded by other equally volatile teenagers. How could it *not* be stressful? On top of all the learning you're made to do, you spend the day dealing with your intense emotional reactions and keeping them in check, so you don't overreact or embarrass yourself.

But your parents don't see any of this happening. So, the question 'How was school?' seems a simple, harmless one, like asking what you had for lunch, or what you watched on TV.

However from your perspective, it's like you've spent the day doing heavy lifting on a treacherous narrow bridge – and now your parents are insisting that you do it all again, just so they can see how you managed it.

Obviously, you don't *want* to do that. But your parents would struggle to grasp why.

We've also seen how the teenage brain is geared towards independence and the rejection of authority, which explains the 'teenage rebel' stereotype. You've maybe seen a lot of this at school, with students who deliberately disrupt lessons just to show that they can.

You may even *be* one of those students. If so, you used to scare me when I was your age, but I'm over it now. Honest!

In any case, the standard teenage brain doesn't respond well to being told what to do.

Of course, school is basically about seven straight hours of being told what to do.

With your brain wired to seek out novelty and new experiences – things that offer immediate rewards, like validation and approval from friends – you're going to struggle when it comes to concentrating on dry, complex educational material.

Luckily, despite the stereotypes, most teenagers *are* able, and often willing, to keep their rebellious, authority-defying impulses under some sort of control. It's just *hard*, is all. So, you should never feel bad for finding school, and learning in general, a struggle. If we're honest, you're doing well to keep at it with a brain that will never be less suited to it.

And besides, at least you can relax and make your own decisions when you get home, right?

Unless, of course, your parents (the main authority figures in your life) are constantly probing you for information, demanding to know what you've been up to.

You've been assessed and ordered around all day at school, so your teenage brain responds poorly to the exact same thing happening at home. As a result, you are very reluctant to tell your parents how your school day went.

Ever been in the middle of something really hard, like constructing a fiddly model, and someone wanders up and says, 'What you doing?' and won't go away until you tell them? It may *seem* like harmless curiosity, but this person is demanding that you sacrifice your time to satisfy their desire to know about something that doesn't involve them. Of course you're going to object to this.

Your parents constantly asking about school can feel a bit like this.

And even if they *do* want to help you with school, these questions can still cause anger and frustration. Humans and their brains are weird like that: even when you don't enjoy it, if you've put time and effort into dealing with something challenging by yourself, you can develop a weird sense of ownership.

This can happen with school: you might not *like* it, but it's *your* job to handle it! This becomes important to you. Your parents butting in with offers of help and assistance can seem like an attempt to deprive you of the little bit of independence you feel you have.

Also, if you're already stressed about something you've put a great deal of work and time into (like school), offers of help can be seriously frustrating. It's like your parents are saying you aren't capable, or that you're doing things wrong, or they don't trust you. This never goes down well.

To demonstrate this to your parents, try helping them drive the car next time you're on a journey. Point out good parking spaces, tell them what speed to go at, warn them about other cars. See how long it takes before they lose patience and get angry.

You know, like *you* do when they keep asking about school.

Another factor to consider, and it's a weird one, is that you're a *different person* at home, around your parents, to the one you are at school. And you want to keep these 'people' separate.

This happens because your brain does many interesting things with the information it has stored. For instance, it quickly recognizes the situations you're in, and automatically knows the right responses.

You know how to behave in a restaurant, right? You also know how to behave at a swimming pool. You also know that these environments are different, so you don't go to restaurants wearing just your underwear or try to swim in the water features.

So good is the brain at keeping information separate from other distinct or *conflicting* information that some people argue that we have *different* selves or identities – that we're *different people* – when we're in different social situations. Especially if they're particularly familiar but distinct situations. Like your school and your home.

I don't mean you're a *completely different* individual in different settings. You're not a Spanish chess player at school, and an angry Australian rapper at home. Your core personality remains the same, but how you behave and respond to things changes.

It's like changing the wallpaper and carpets in a room; the room will stay the same size and shape, but it will *look* very different to anyone who sees it.

The point is, you think, behave and react in a certain way at school, and you think, behave and react in a different way at home. The expectations placed on you are different, you're around different people of different ages, so of course the 'you' you are at home is not the same 'you' as the 'you' you are at school.[28]

This happens with your parents too. Do you think they behave the same way at home as they do when they're working? If your mother is, say, a doctor, do you think she wanders around the hospital telling patients to get out of bed and badgering them for not tidying their bandages? Let's hope not.

So, you're a different type of person in different settings. That's how your brain does things. But it can be difficult and distressing if you're in a situation where you have to combine these personalities.

---

28. Apologies for the number of times I said 'you' in this sentence. Got a bit carried away.

Have you bumped into a teacher while out with your parents or friends? It's really *weird*, and uncomfortable, isn't it?

This is partly because you never see teachers outside school, so you assume they must live there (maybe they sleep upright in the stationery cupboard, like some boring vampire?), but it's *also* because who you are around your teacher is *not* who you are around your parents or friends. Dealing with both at the same time means you've got two separate sets of well-established rules battling it out in your head.

It's like having two favourite TV shows. One is a wacky animated comedy, the other a drama with dragons and axes and blood. Both are fine, but if the sarcastic talking horse from the first started popping up in the realistic, brutal battle scenes of the second, it would be seriously confusing, and probably ruin both.

That's sort of what your parents are inadvertently doing when they probe you about school when you get home.

They're trying to talk to 'school you', but you're 'home you' right now. You've finished watching one TV programme and have moved on to the next, but they keep trying to put the first one back on, and this causes issues.

And what if that first programme is one you'd rather your parents *didn't know about*? Let's be honest, you've said things about your parents at school that you wouldn't *dare* at home, right? You've mocked the stupid things they said, you've rolled your eyes at their ridiculous demands, you've sworn about your most recent falling-out.

And why not? Your parents *aren't there* at school. That's the point. And moaning about, or making fun of, your parents is a key part of being a teenager. It's something you all have in common, and it can be incredibly satisfying to voice all the thoughts and resentments you build up but can't express at home.

But it does mean that your brain tries to keep 'school you' as far away from your parents as possible. Who knows what they might say?

There's nothing wrong happening here, by the way.

It's perfectly healthy, even *necessary,* behaviour.

You think your parents don't do it? Even the most dedicated parent will have conversations at work or with friends about all the dumb and annoying stuff you say and do. Some people talk about little else.

It's quite ironic, but one of the things teenagers and their parents have in common is **an enthusiasm for moaning about each other**.

All this means that you are annoyed when your parents want to know about what's going on with you at school. Teenagers are especially vulnerable to school stresses, given that their brains are undergoing so much upheaval; getting away from school concerns is especially important, as it allows for recovery time.

Interference from your parents, even if it's well meant, deprives you of this escape, reducing your capacity to think and function, even to the point where you're maxed out.

It also creates a negative association between school and your parents. So, any desire to address school stuff with them in a useful way is quickly quashed by your parents' actions.

To put it simply, their efforts to engage with your school progress could make you *do worse* at school.

And yet they can't stop asking. **Will they never learn?**

TROUBLESHOOTING

THE PROBLEM: **Parents amplify the stress of school**, either by dismissing or downplaying what you're experiencing, or by attempting to discuss it, or involve themselves in your progress.

THE CONSEQUENCES: **All this stress will impact on your schooling in negative ways.**

THE SOLUTIONS: **As with anything else**, just knowing what's going on can help reduce the stress.

1 **Students who seemingly like and enjoy school don't appear to get as stressed** (not outwardly, anyway) or rebellious: one explanation is that they feel they *have independence*, because they *want* to be there.

So, if there's something at school you *do* like and *are* good at, focus on it, and try to improve at that. This could provide a sense of independence and control that you otherwise lack. It certainly won't solve *everything*, but such things are known to reduce stress and improve well-being.

2 **Calmly explaining matters**, in a 'here's why that bothers me' way, could diffuse some issues.

Sometimes some simple rephrasing can make a big difference. If your parents ask you how school went when you're not in the mood, instead of refusing or closing down the discussion with 'fine', maybe try asking, 'Is it OK if we talk about it later?'

That way, you get to retain control of the conversation, and your parents feel involved and included. You're not shutting them out, you're rescheduling. Sure, you do still have to talk about it with them, but as and when *you* feel up to it.

And who knows, your parents may be able to help. Anything that makes the school experience better is probably worth considering. They're the best days of your life, after all!

Of course, if you *do* experience a lot of stress at school, it can be a real problem for your state of mind . . .

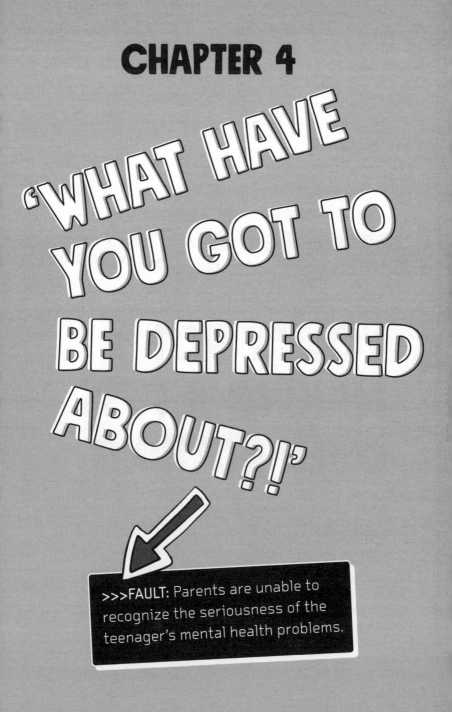

CHAPTER 4

'WHAT HAVE YOU GOT TO BE DEPRESSED ABOUT?!'

>>>FAULT: Parents are unable to recognize the seriousness of the teenager's mental health problems.

Have you felt very anxious or nervous about things lately? Is the idea of doing simple, familiar things, like catching a bus or going to school, suddenly filling you with apprehension and dread in a way it hasn't before?

Or maybe you just feel really down. You can't muster up any enthusiasm about *anything* and each day seems like trudging through knee-deep grey porridge.

YOU'RE NOT MAKING A FUSS OVER NOTHING

So far, we've spoken about your parents, and the arguments you have with them, as if they're just an irritation – an annoying problem to be managed and worked around while rolling your eyes and sighing.[29]

---

29. Pretty much every parenting guide talks about *you* as if you're a mindless obstacle, like a cow that's wandered on to a motorway. Why not return the favour?

This is because, as we've seen, often there are ways to make things better.

But it's important to recognize that it doesn't always stop at that. The friction and stress we've seen in the previous chapters (whether they're caused by your parents, your own development or the pressures of modern life) – they don't just magically go away. Sometimes they can have a big impact on your ability to function normally.

This is true for everyone, but especially for teenagers. And it can be made worse by the fact that parents and teenagers view things in very different ways.[30]

Adults can often make fun of this – of teenagers being closed off or unsociable, sitting alone in a darkened room, wearing all-black clothes and listening to bleak or angry music.

---

30. What definitely *doesn't* help is parents nagging you to 'get out of the house' or 'go and see your friends', or saying you're 'always moping' or have a 'face like a wet weekend'.

But if everything makes you anxious or miserable, why *wouldn't* you stay in your safe, familiar room and embrace things that reflect your mood?

Occasionally, some unthinking parents will ask:

'WHAT HAVE *YOU* GOT TO BE DEPRESSED ABOUT?'

Firstly, all joking aside, this can be one of *the most harmful things* an adult can say to you – to the point where your *life* could be at risk. Most parents would be horrified to hear this. They clearly don't mean to do you harm. But the problem is, you're *not* making a big deal out of nothing, and anyone insisting that you are just makes things worse.

You might think, *Isn't that a bit extreme?* It's not *nice* to have your parents (or anyone) say that to you, but it's still just words. Remember that saying about sticks and stones?

I'm not being over the top, though. They might be just words, but they're *dangerous* words.

Because they have a serious effect on something incredibly important.

Your mental health.

WHAT IS MENTAL HEALTH?

It's how well you process, cope, think about, respond to and interact with everything in your life, both consciously and emotionally. It's what pretty much defines *who you can be*.

Teenagers are particularly vulnerable, or at risk, when it comes to developing mental health problems – especially anxiety or depression, with many teenagers showing signs of *both*!

Despite what many parents claim, teenagers aren't just being lazy or melodramatic; **they may be struggling with genuine mental health difficulties**.

Think about the beginning of this chapter. Being nervous and paranoid all the time? That's basically what anxiety is. And feeling perpetually unhappy and completely lacking in enthusiasm? That's depression.

It's perfectly normal to experience these feelings sometimes, but when you *can't stop*, when your mind seems to be stuck in this state for days, weeks, months on end, *that's* when something's wrong. And it can be more *likely* to happen to teenagers.

Why? Well, lots of reasons. Everything affects your mental health, like your home environment, your sleep and school. **And all of us experience them differently.**

However, one key factor is your relationship with your parents.

There are many ways for your parents to make your mental health worse, without meaning to. But then there are also ways they can make it *better*, or even be the ones who keep it intact.

That's why it's *so important* to make the effort to understand each other and get along as much as possible. Let's look at why mental health is important, why your parents may struggle to understand this, and then see what we can do to fix that.

WHY IS EVERYONE SO OBSESSED WITH MENTAL HEALTH?

Mental health problems probably aren't unfamiliar to you. Just as you know more about modern music and online culture than your parents (and most adults), you probably *know more about mental health*.

It's regularly addressed at school, and appears online via articles or hashtags or memes, thanks to ongoing efforts to encourage people to be more open about mental health issues; even celebrities have become involved in the conversation. So you're probably used to hearing terms like social phobia, or depression.

You're also probably aware of things like anxiety, eating disorders, of people being down or manic. Maybe you've heard of someone having a wobble, or an off day, and understand these as ways to describe periods of poor mental health.

A lot of mental health campaigns are directed at teenagers because, as we've seen, you're more vulnerable to mental health problems.

Honestly, don't you have *enough* to deal with already? **Yes, you do. That's part of the problem.**

But in order to explain this, let's look at *how* mental health can go wrong.

WHAT HAPPENS WHEN MENTAL HEALTH GOES WRONG?

Your mental health is the result of all the countless complex processes in your brain.

It's impressive, but it also means there are many ways in which *something can go wrong*.

It may be something biological. A glitch in your DNA, too much or too little of a certain brain chemical can produce a chain reaction that causes mental health problems, just as one software bug can crash an entire operating system.

It doesn't have to be something physical. Mental health can also suffer as a result of negative, unpleasant *experiences*. Poor education, living in poverty or in high-crime areas, traumatic incidents (like assault, or involvement in violence) – all sorts of unpleasant experiences can seriously hamper mental health.

Because our brains are involved in *everything we do*, mental health problems can be affected by countless different issues. Working out the exact cause is often like throwing a laptop down a massive flight of stairs and trying to figure out which specific step actually broke it. Not easy.

Mental health issues are often hideously complicated, so they can quickly become **overwhelming, and scary**.

A useful way of approaching mental health is to use something called the stress–vulnerability model. This diagram might look complicated, but it basically shows that the more vulnerable you are or feel, the less stress it takes to trigger symptoms of poor mental health.

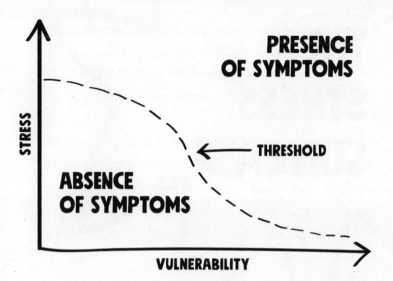

Remember, stress has real negative effects on your brain *and* your body. Also, *any* unpleasant experience or difficulty can cause stress, placing more demands, physical and mental, on your brain, forcing it to work even harder.

However, your brain can only cope with so much stress. If it's exposed to *more than it can handle*, normal operations break down. The results of stress spill over into everything else, gumming up the works and causing multiple problems.

And what happens? Your mental health suffers . . .

THE STRESS SUITCASE

It's like packing a suitcase. A suitcase has a limited amount of space in it. Stay within that limit, it works fine.

But if you insist on jamming in more stuff than it can hold, eventually the catch will snap off, the hinges will break, the seams will burst, and you end up with a suitcase that doesn't work *at all*.

Your brain is like that suitcase. Stress is the stuff you pack into it. It doesn't matter if it's one thing, like a

bulky ski jacket (the stress of a major trauma, such as a car crash) or lots of little things like balled-up socks (the many small, persistent stresses of your life). Too much is too much, and the suitcase won't hold it all.

However, suitcases come in many different sizes. Similarly, not every brain can absorb stress in the same way. Exactly *how much stress* you can endure depends on elements of your biology and development, but it determines how *vulnerable* you are to mental health problems. If you can absorb a lot of stress, you're not very vulnerable. If you can't take on much at all, you are.

It's worth remembering that if someone can't handle much stress it's usually not because they're weak, but because they've *experienced so much* already. Their brain's constantly working to keep it under control. They may have a big suitcase, but someone's half filled it with useless bricks.

It is
emotional baggage
you're carrying
around with you.

That's how the stress–vulnerability model works: it considers how much stress you're *dealing with*, combined with how much stress you can *cope with*. Both are crucial in whether or not you become mentally unwell.

Unfortunately, there are so many things that cause stress: school commitments, falling out with friends, low self-esteem, pressures to succeed and be liked, physical injuries, harassment.

Also, not everyone reacts to things in the same way.

Some people go to pieces when they've got loads of work and a looming deadline, others thrive under pressure. Some find a messy house unbearable, others don't mind it at all, but *are* stressed by being made to clean up.

It also depends on how sensitive you are to problems and difficulties. Or how well your brain can process them.

We've all met people who make a drama out of every minor crisis. While some may just be exaggerating to gain attention, others may be experiencing powerful, confusing emotional reactions in response to seemingly minor issues, *especially* if their mental suitcase is already full.

Basically, we're *all* vulnerable to mental health problems, but you're even *more* vulnerable if your brain has a limited capacity to handle stress. Or produces overly powerful emotions. Or struggles to deal with unpleasant experiences.

You're *especially* vulnerable if your brain does *all those things*. You know, like the typical teenage brain does.

WHY IS MENTAL HEALTH SO RISKY FOR *YOU*?

So, when it comes to mental health, teenagers get a pretty raw deal.

But *don't panic*. Most teenagers don't end up with anxiety, depression or some other disorder. It's just that, for some, the *chances* of doing so are higher than for most other people.

Mental health is like riding a bike, and an episode of poor mental health is like falling off it.

No matter how good you are at riding a bike, it's always *possible* to fall off. But it's easier for some to fall off than others. Some have bikes that need repair and maintenance, others are riding over rough terrain, and so on.

Teenagers? You're riding a hastily assembled bike along a winding, icy mountain path. You still have a decent chance of staying on your bike, but if *anyone's* going to fall off . . .

Why do you have to take the treacherous route, while most adults stay on the nice smooth tarmac?

Well, we've already seen how much extra work your teenage brain is doing as it changes and matures.[31] But this workload leaves less space in your brain for dealing with problems that cause (and are caused by) stress. It's as if your suitcase has a bowling ball in it. That's not great for mental health.

Also, as mentioned way back in chapter one, in your case the regions of the brain responsible for managing and processing emotional reactions are still developing.

31. That's why you need that extra sleep, which you rarely get.

Meanwhile the parts responsible for emotions and impulses are fired up and ready to go.

So, you experience much *stronger* and harder-to-control emotional reactions to practically *everything*. And not all emotions are good. Many are deeply unpleasant, causing more stress.

However, these powerful emotions **can be essential**.

Your developing brain needs to figure out how to handle these upgraded emotions, so it has to *experience* them. Otherwise it's like training to be a pilot without being allowed in an aeroplane: difficult, to say the least.

But, because it's still learning, sometimes your brain *can't* deliver the appropriate emotional response.

If someone broke up with you at a party, you'd feel upset and angry; perhaps you'd feel lonely and jealous of the person they're seeing now. Or, if your backpack split, spilling all your schoolwork into a puddle, you'd *definitely* feel frustrated. But maybe you'd laugh at the situation too?

While unpleasant experiences trigger reactions in many regions of the brain, the more sophisticated parts of the brain gather up all these reactions and translate them into feelings and emotions we recognize. They take all the mixed-up stuff in your brain and make sense of it.

Take a range of separate sounds and, individually, they may not mean anything. It's just noise. But put them together? Your brain can recognize the whole as a specific song.

However, because your brain is still developing, you often struggle to do this, or simply find it *impossible*. So when something bad happens you *may not know how to feel*. Or respond. Your brain basically throws up an ERROR message.

ERROR!

Although it's totally normal, being unable to articulate your feelings can cause serious frustration, meaning *more* stress.

This problem is worse if you're someone who bottles things up. Constantly suppressing your emotions and moods means that your developing brain is denied the chance to learn how to process them properly. And, if your brain already struggles to deal with negative emotions, it doesn't take much to overwhelm it.

Unfortunately, many things discourage teenagers from expressing their feelings: strict parenting, the need to be cool and in control, and other pressures from an often critical society.

Over time, this can dramatically increase the risk of emotional dysfunction (a reduced ability to deal with and process emotions) and mood disorders.

This is why it's wrong for anyone to criticize teenagers for being 'emotional'.

It's essential that you're allowed to express your feelings.

SOUND THE ALARM!

Your brain has what's known as a 'threat-detection system', an ancient but vital neurological network that monitors everything going on in your brain. When it identifies something that might lead to unpleasantness, it sounds the alarm, alerting us that something dangerous is, or could be, about to happen.

It's *this* part of the brain which decides that stress is a valid reaction. We've talked a little bit about things that can stress you out at school, but we need to look at this in more detail now. Because stress is an offshoot of that very familiar and powerful emotion – *fear*!

Stress is more common, but less intense, than fear, although they are linked. Fear is like the big bad boss in a movie or video game, and stress represents all the henchmen that have to be fought off before the epic final battle. But they all work together, because both stress and fear are triggered by our brain's threat-detection system.

However, modern humans, with our powerful brains, recognize countless different types of threat, because so many things *can* make us feel bad.

Failing an exam? Asking someone out on a date? Being told off by your parents? Leaving your phone on the bus? All these, and way more, are recognized by your threat-detection system as dangers to be avoided like something with big teeth lurking in the shadows. That's why they *all cause stress*.

Especially during your teenage years. Your threat-detection system is also maturing and you're becoming more aware of consequences and big-picture stuff, so you have more things to worry about.

Thankfully, our brains eventually figure out that most things aren't *that* dangerous, so there's no need for full-blown panic at the very idea of them. But, as this is another complex higher-brain function, figuring it out takes *time*.

This may explain why younger teenagers are so often seen as shy, nervous and awkward. Indeed, levels of anxiety are at their highest in the first few years of your teens (around ages ten to thirteen), after which they usually decline, because by then the sophisticated parts of your brain have learned that most of the alarms from the threat-detection system *aren't necessary*, and tunes them out.

For example, just now I mentioned the idea of asking someone out, something many teenagers genuinely *fear*. Logically, there's no reason for this: the person you're talking to isn't going to physically harm you in any way.[32] And yet the very *idea* can cause nausea-inducing stress.

But, from your perspective, your fear is justified.

Let's just deal with the awkwardness: a key part of being a teenager is that you're becoming sexually mature. All the processes concerned with sex and reproduction – both physical and mental – are coming online, thanks to all those hormones flooding your system.

---

32. Unless you're attempting to chat up a leopard (which, if you're not a leopard, would be seriously weird).

It's already a confusing, chaotic time. Unfortunately, nature is a real jerk here. You've gone from thinking

You're suddenly finding a lot of the people around you, even the ones who've been getting on your nerves for years, intensely desirable in unfamiliar, confusing ways. But this happens while your changing body is gifting you acne, greasy hair, and *new* hair in places where there wasn't any before. And that's if it's the opposite sex you're attracted to. This also applies if you're attracted to the same sex, but with an added level of stress given how many people still aren't OK with this. We'll explore this more later.

All at once, you find others very attractive, and this at a time when you've never been less confident about your own appearance. It's no wonder that talking to someone you fancy can cause panic and stress. So, you avoid them. It just makes sense.

But then, one day, you summon the courage to say 'hello'. Just hello. And they say 'hello' back. This doesn't *mean* anything; you're not suddenly dating, it's simply basic manners. However, it gives your developing brain *something to work with.*

You spoke to someone attractive, and *nothing bad happened.* So, next time your threat-detection systems start blaring at the prospect of speaking to an attractive person, your sensible brain can go, 'I've *done that* before, and I didn't burst into flames. This fear response is nonsense, I'll ignore it.'

The threat-detection, anxiety-causing regions of your brain go up a gear once you reach your teens. However, you gradually gain experiences, which helps your brain to control (and ignore) them better; and so anxiety declines as you get older.

Unfortunately, this sort of learning and development is less likely to take place if your anxiety is *so strong* that you avoid everything and everyone and stay in your room. Your brain cannot experience anything that teaches it to ignore the over-the-top fear responses, so they stay fresh and powerful. Full-blown anxiety occurs when this goes too far, and your brain ends up fearing pretty much *everything*. It saves time.

It's hardly surprising that so many teenagers struggle with mental health issues. **It's more surprising that so many of you *don't*.**

PART OF
THE GANG

We've seen that talking to someone you fancy can be a stressful experience. And thanks to your sexual development, you're suddenly and inexplicably attracted to *a lot* of people, so that's *a lot* of stress.

But here's the thing: it doesn't even have to be anything 'sexual' for you to feel high levels of stress when interacting with others your own age. It can happen with anyone. And everyone.

Peer pressure, bullying, popularity, fitting in, being accepted: these are all things that cause *tremendous* pressure for teenagers, with serious implications for your mental health.

Why, though? Saying that teenagers crave independence, but also desperately want everyone to like them – isn't that a bit of a contradiction?

But that's just how people work.

Humans are an *incredibly* social species.

Think of your school assembly: hundreds of young people, sitting quietly in the same room. Our closest evolutionary relatives, chimpanzees, *can't do that.* You put fifty chimps in a room, and they'll quickly start screaming and fighting. There'll be blood and poo everywhere within minutes.[33]

But we humans *like* having others around us. We're *wired* to seek the approval and respect of other people. It's a key part of who we are, how we think.

This need occurs at the deepest levels of our brains. Having a nice interaction with someone, even if it's just a smile and a nod, triggers activity in our old friend the reward pathway.

Having a positive interaction with someone **causes pleasure in our brains**.

---

33. Although I don't know your school – maybe that is how your assemblies usually end up?

That's why you can hang around with your friends for hours, just talking about unimportant things, yet still enjoy it. Everyone getting along is a real kick for the human brain.

Remember, that's why so many teenagers end up messing about with friends rather than paying attention during lessons. Your education may be important, but it's often not much fun. Interacting with your friends? *That's* fun. As we've seen, your still-maturing brain prefers things that offer immediate rewards, rather than benefits later (like getting a good education, meaning better prospects as an adult). It's a constant battle for teenagers, resisting unhelpful choices that are immediately enjoyable.

Similarly, a 'negative social interaction', such as being rejected, causes distress, even *pain*. This isn't physical pain from an injury, but it's processed in the same area of the brain. We definitely don't like it.

Even something trivial, like being ignored or dismissed by a stranger, can trigger distress in the brain. We *crave* acceptance. Not from everyone, but from groups or communities we feel part of. Like our circle of friends, or any teams we belong to.

It's not just about being *liked*, though. **We need to be respected, looked up to.**

We need status, to feel superior, accomplished in some way. It often doesn't matter how. Maybe you have the best clothes, are better at a sport or at exams, can fit the most marshmallows in your mouth . . . Whatever. What matters is that you get to feel you're good, better or best at *something*.

Our self-esteem – our idea of how successful a person we are – is a vital part of our personality. It keeps us motivated, gives us confidence in our decisions, *maintains our well-being and mental health*. It's something many teenagers struggle with, and it comes from comparing ourselves to other people, even if we don't realize we're doing it.

Unfortunately, this competition can lead to unpleasantness. A shortcut to status, to feeling superior, is to tear someone else down, make them *inferior*. This is what triggers bullying and harassment, especially of people who are different or stand out in some way. By publicly highlighting their flaws you get to feel superior and accepted by others.

This also helps to explain why bullies so often have difficult lives themselves. They crave status and acceptance more than most, and resort to unpleasant methods to get it.

Sadly, individuals who occupy the lowest position in a group, who are the butt of everyone's jokes, experience severe stress, even disorders. Anti-bullying campaigns exist for a reason.

To recap: humans *need* acceptance and approval from others. So much so that our brains have developed tactics to increase the chances of people liking us, to boost our self-esteem.

RESPECT

Some scientists refer to 'impression management', which is when we instinctively present the best possible image of ourselves to those around us. We big-up our achievements and downplay our flaws, and try to make other people like us. Even if we don't care about them, we do whatever we can to look or sound our best.

Heck, so important is our self-esteem that we even *lie to ourselves*. We convince ourselves that we're right, good, cool and worthwhile, even if nobody else appreciates us.

Some people take this too far. How else do you explain those contestants on reality-TV talent contests? The ones convinced they're going to be megastars when their singing voice sounds like a bag of cats in a washing machine.

Of course, mocking them *makes us* feel superior, boosting our self-esteem, which is part of the appeal.[34]

Everybody has this basic *need* to be liked and respected, **but it's about ten times stronger in teenagers like you**.

Your new desire for independence means that your most reliable relationship, the one with your parents, is suddenly uncertain, tense, even distressing. So, you seek connections, approval and reliable relationships elsewhere.

That's why bonding with others your age becomes so important during your teens. All the stuff you feel you're no longer getting from your parents (reassurance, approval, support, etc.) you need from friends and peers; impressing them and gaining their approval is *vital*. Your mental health may depend on it.

34. For the record, I think these shows are dreadful, for this very reason.

Many people wonder why teenagers are so obsessed with popularity at school. Well, this is often the reason.

It's also why you tend to ignore your parents' concerns about you falling in with a bad crowd. You instinctively seek *more* approval from your peers and *less* approval from your parents, so *their* concerns are going to be less important to you.

However, your parents are often right to be concerned. Who are the people from whom you seek friendship and approval? They're also teenagers, so they're prone to the same problems as you – like a tendency to choose immediate rewards over sensible restraint, which may lead to dabbling with drugs and alcohol.

Maybe this also explains why teenage best friends can have blazing rows or full-on fist fights over bizarrely minor things, but the next day act as if nothing has happened?

It's good that teenage bonds can be so flexible, but it brings yet *more* stress to your life: the dull-but-reliable bond with your parents is replaced by the fun-yet-unpredictable ones with your peers.

Is it any wonder that teenagers are so often anxious about talking to others, especially new people?

Being liked and accepted is incredibly important for you, **so being rejected is really distressing**.

It never ends, does it?

WHY DO PARENTS STRUGGLE WITH TAKING *YOUR* MENTAL HEALTH SERIOUSLY?

How do your parents affect your mental health? What can they do or say when you start to falter? And why are their reactions sometimes quite unhelpful, even harmful?

Remember, *you probably know more about mental health than your parents*. That's a big deal. It's only been discussed with younger people for the past couple of decades. You've grown up exposed to the concept, while your parents almost certainly didn't.

This often means that your mental health (and how things affect it) is something that simply *doesn't occur to them*. That's not just a problem for you. It's a problem with mental health generally: you can't see what's going on inside someone's head, so it's harder to recognize that they're experiencing difficulties.

If your mental health isn't something they consider, your parents might see you being anxious or moody and think it's easily fixed. You're just being timid, or self-indulgent, and need to be snapped out of it with some tough love!

Funnily enough, this sort of approach rarely helps.

Let's go back to that anxiety about speaking to someone (maybe you fancy or admire them). Some parents will 'playfully' mock you or dismiss your worries, saying 'Don't be daft' or 'They won't bite' – after all, how dangerous can it be, just saying hello to someone?

But here again, your brain is operating very differently from your parents'. Remember, embarrassment and the fear of being rejected hits you *way harder* than it does your parents. So, them telling you there's 'nothing to worry about', *that's wrong*.

It's like they're stroking a friendly pet dog, like a spaniel, and telling you to do the same with another nearby dog, because it's clearly safe.

Except that the one you have to stroke *isn't* a playful dog.

It's a wolf.
Which looks really hungry.

Sure, it *could* be safe to pet, but if it isn't, you're going to seriously regret it. However, your parents just see 'friendly dog' and pester you into doing it, despite the stress it's causing you.

THIS ISN'T BECAUSE YOUR PARENTS DON'T CARE

Many problems stem from them caring too much.

Your parents want to be *good* parents, to do right by you. But other parents can be *very* harsh judges when it comes to how they're raising you. Trust me on this.

This pressure to be a good parent (often the same kind of pressure that makes teenagers obsess about popularity at school) can lead to concerns about their child being unhappy.

If you're a good parent, then your child should be happy, right? If they're not, either something's wrong with them, or *you're* doing something wrong as a parent. Either way, you need to *fix* it. We saw this earlier regarding your school progress.

Except . . . that's *not how people work*! Nobody should be happy all the time.

The idea that if you're not happy then you're failing in some way is a creation of the modern world. **And it's *wrong*! And often harmful.**

I JUST WANT YOU TO BE HAPPY.

IT'S LIKE YOU EVEN WANT TO CONTROL MY FEELINGS NOW!

Of course, you care about your parents' feelings too. Any mention of you being unhappy upsets them, so you'll want to *stop telling them*. So you bottle things up. Which we know isn't brilliant.

Moreover, if your parents have worked hard to care and provide for you, then your unhappiness may seem like a *rejection* of all their efforts. If your parents are already dealing with serious stresses of their own, they may accuse you of being melodramatic, ungrateful and spoilt and insist you snap out of it.

Whatever the cause, this is a dangerous thing to say to a teenager.

All your issues –
your stress,
your emotions,
your rock-bottom self-esteem
and your mental health
problems –
have been dismissed.

All this anxiety and distress you're feeling because you think you're a crappy, flawed person? Your parents *have confirmed it*! They've made it clear that your issues have no value and that you're pathetic for thinking otherwise.

While it's highly unlikely they *mean* that, what's it going to do for your already fragile self-esteem?

We've seen that problems occur when your parents do or say things that discourage you from being open and honest about your feelings, or mental health. And, unfortunately, there are so many things that can lead them to do this.

This is not a good situation. It means you feel compelled to endure your problems, to wait them out and hope they go away, or to keep them suppressed, under wraps. Again, this usually makes things worse, not better.

Any division between you and your parents is also unhelpful because they often play a *crucial* role in managing and treating your mental health problems.

They are the ones who can provide the care, support and encouragement you need if you're grappling with issues like this. Having them onside means you don't have to go it alone and experiment with more dangerous methods in order to feel better.

Teenagers may end up dabbling in drugs or alcohol because they just want some relief from their problems. But such relief is short-lived and gives your struggling brain even more to deal with.

Teenagers with mental health issues are also more likely to engage in self-harm, which can be distressing and dangerous.[35]

No one should feel ashamed about doing it, but it's important to seek help as there's a risk that you will cause lasting physical damage to yourself – or even death. It's no surprise that the thought of self-harming freaks out parents and others who care about you.

That's the thing about mental health problems: they *stop you thinking rationally*. That's the point. It's hard to worry about what people who care about you will think when you believe that *nobody cares about you*. You end up believing ideas that are seriously *bad*.

Just to confirm: *they are seriously bad!*

35. This is properly serious stuff, so if you need any information or advice, skip to page 320 where there is a list of contacts for issues raised in the book.

But thinking rationally is a struggle for teenagers at the best of times, given how your brain is still working things out. That's why you tend to take more risks, and be more rebellious. If you're in the grip of disrupted mental health *as well*? That just makes things worse.

Your brain is still developing, and the changes you experience during your teenage years are meant to serve you through adulthood, so mental health problems that develop and go unresolved during teenage years risk causing problems later in life too.

They need not be permanent and persistent – your life's not automatically ruined – but you can remain vulnerable to reccurrences for many years to come.

Failure to address or acknowledge your mental health issues may make your relationship with your parents even more tense and unstable, driving you further apart, which just makes things even harder and compounds the problems.

To avoid all this, what you'd need is someone looking out for you; someone who *can* think logically and rationally, who seriously cares, more than anything, about your health and well-being, and who you can trust.

In other words,
a parent.

But it's a two-way thing. Having supportive, engaged parents can make all the difference when it comes to counteracting mental health problems. Or *avoiding* them, if your relationship is already reasonably healthy.

But parents often struggle to comprehend and cope with your issues.

Finding out that your child is mentally unwell, when you don't know much about mental health? Your child is ill, but you can't do anything directly to fix it (aspirin and chicken soup aren't much use here), you don't really know *what's happening*, and you feel it may even be *your fault*.

This is a nightmare scenario for parents, so there's a good chance they'll react very strongly to it.

And this is where a strong, open relationship between you and your parents is so important.

They can help and support you when you need it most, **and you can explain and reassure them about what's going on**.

All things that are much easier to do if you're not wasting time arguing about things that definitely *don't* matter. If you've removed wet towels, bedtime and homework from the argument list, you'll have a lot more space and energy to talk about the stuff that matters.

TROUBLESHOOTING

THE PROBLEM: **A teenager's mental health is particularly vulnerable**, and your ability to think rationally and make decisions is not at full strength yet, so you often end up engaging in thinking and behaviours that may make the problem worse.

Your parents can be a huge help here, but if your relationship is already quite tense and you aren't getting on, they can make things worse, even if they're trying to help.

THE CONSEQUENCES: **Mental health problems can be very serious if left untreated.**

THE SOLUTIONS

1 **Firstly, always remember that being mentally unwell does not mean that you're a flawed or inferior person in any way** – any more than falling off your bike means that you're incapable of riding one.

2 **It's fine to not be happy all the time.** The idea that, if you're not happy, then something's wrong is a modern misconception, and an unhealthy one. Your parents might buy into it, but that doesn't mean it's right. Of course they'd rather you were happy. But they should also appreciate that it's not *essential*.

It's *fine* to be unhappy, angry, anxious – anything like that. It becomes a problem when you *can't stop* feeling like that for no obvious reason.

3 **A healthy diet can help with mental health issues.** It's tempting to indulge in junk food or sugary energy drinks to make yourself feel better, but relief is brief: such a diet will make you less healthy, and you may feel worse. A bad diet may disrupt your sleep, which is often an essential part of effective self-care (taking action to maintain or improve your health).

4 **Regular exercise is often linked to improved mental health.** It makes sense: your brain is an organ that depends on your body, and the healthier your body is, the more your brain can do and cope with, because the fitter body can sustain it better.

5 **Mental health problems, by definition, affect how you think about and react to things.** It's a big ask, but if you're suffering from a mental health problem try to be aware that your thoughts and views will be affected by it. You may think that everything is scary, or that nothing matters and everything's awful, but that could be the issues talking, not you. Take a few moments to question your first instincts.

6 **A large majority of mental health problems in teenagers can be treated without medication**, and counselling tends to be reasonably effective. But there are stubborn cases where medication like antidepressants is required. Many parents are deeply suspicious of such medication, but it's a vital tool in combating mental health problems. Be sure to follow the advice you're given: advice based on evidence and clinical practice, not misinformation or suspicion.

Because they're so complex and variable, there are many different approaches to tackling mental health problems, and it's often a matter of finding one that works for you. If you do some research online, follow the advice about using the internet you've had at school. Be aware that not everyone has the best intentions. If something sounds too good to be true, *it usually is*, especially if it involves you buying something. Where possible, stick to confirmed sources, like the NHS, the World Health Organization and certified therapists.

7 **Reducing conflict in your relationship with your parents can be great for preserving your mental health.** Having some common ground helps, so try to keep in mind that your parents are probably experiencing the same stresses and pressures as you, just in different ways – many of which stem from caring for, and about, you.

However, this can be difficult for everyone. Your parents are meant to be the ones with greater experience, while you crave control and independence, so asking for help goes against the grain. But working through this resistance can be a vital step that benefits everyone.

Remember that, while your parents can play a vital part in managing mental health problems and preventing you from resorting to drastic, dangerous solutions, they probably aren't as clued up about mental health as you are. They may need guidance – and reassurance that this isn't a major calamity that is all their doing. You may even want to show them useful websites and resources. You're never too old to learn.

8 **However, sometimes it's better to talk to someone you *don't* know about your mental health concerns.** You may feel too close to your parents – there's too much going on. Reaching out to a trusted friend, a reliable teacher or school counsellor, or even just a sympathetic stranger in one of the official online mental health communities (there are many), can be a helpful first step in dealing with your mental health issues. If the idea of telling your parents is daunting, try talking to someone who isn't so close to things. They may be able to help you get to the point where you're ready and able to talk about it with your family.

A lot of the time, it comes down to you and your parents helping *each other*.

There are always resources available if you want to know more, especially online. However, that leads to another issue . . .

CHAPTER 5

'CAN YOU GET OFF THAT PHONE FOR ONE MINUTE!'

>>>FAULT: Parents are obsessed with how much time the teenager spends on their device!

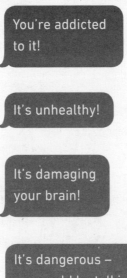

We've seen how arguments happen when you're at home. We've seen how arguments happen about school.[36]

What you need is some space.

Unfortunately, putting some space between yourself and your parents is tricky. Our world has many laws and rules and costs and, crucially, age restrictions, so teenagers have very limited options for getting out of the house.

That's why it's so infuriating when your parents say, 'While you're under my roof, you'll obey my rules!' You've *no choice* about living under their roof – you're not allowed to live anywhere else!

And even when you *do* have somewhere else to go (like a friend's house, or the park, or the local McDonald's), parents always demand to know where you're going and why, when you'll be back, or insist on taking you there, when the whole point of going is *getting away from them*.

And parents really don't like you using your home as

---

36. I mean, we've even seen how arguments happen when you're asleep.

somewhere to sleep, coming and going as you please. (Something that leads to accusations of treating the house like a hotel, remember?)

So, if you're in the house, your parents get annoyed and argue with you. And if you're not in the house, your parents get annoyed and argue with you. You can't win! All you can do to avoid arguments is just stay at home and sit in silence.

This isn't a useful solution, because you're not a pot plant.

You *need* stimulation, *need* independence, *need* to socialize, **to explore the world on your own terms**.

Well, thanks to technology, we now have smartphones, tablets, laptops, games consoles, Wi-Fi and all that stuff! These are a godsend for teenagers, allowing you to explore the online world, meet and interact with other people, experience new and stimulating things, even find out information for your schoolwork. All at the touch of a button, and under your complete control.

These are things that your chaotic, maturing brain is crying out for!

Best of all, you can do this all *from home*. While you're just sat there. *Quietly.* So, this must please your parents, right?

Er . . . no!

Parents have a whole arsenal of concerns and criticisms when it comes to you spending time with your favourite device.

But your phone[37] is your link to the universe outside your house. If your parents try to interfere with it, or even take it away . . . you're not going to react well to that!

Before you know it **BOOM!** More arguments.

---

37. To keep things simple, I'm going to focus on smartphones, but much of what I say about them is just as valid for tablets, laptops, consoles and so on.

This is another example of how you and your parents think and feel completely differently about the *same thing*. *They* view your smartphone with suspicion, even fear. *You* feel the exact opposite: it's essential entertainment, a tool, a status symbol and a social lifeline, all rolled into one.

But . . . who's right? The media are always going on about the dangers of smartphones and your parents are constantly throwing these warnings at you, but is there any *truth* to these claims? Are you slowly killing yourself by using a smartphone? Or are those worries just products of suspicion, paranoia and old-fashioned nagging?

Let's take a look.

'AM I "ADDICTED" TO MY PHONE?'

Addiction is a very serious condition. It's mentioned a lot when people talk about smartphone use. But it *shouldn't* be.

True addiction rewires your brain, compelling you to seek out the thing you're addicted to (usually a drug, but it can be an activity, like gambling), even to the extent of ignoring or dismissing important things (friends, family, laws) in order to get it. Often, you *can't function* without it. Your brain has been altered to the point where you genuinely *need* it.

To date, there's no official record of anyone being unable to function (physically or mentally) if you take away their smartphone. So, smartphones don't seem to be truly addictive, whatever parents claim.

However, smartphones *do* seem to lead to obsessive behaviour, where you're *compelled* to check or use it, no matter what's going on around you. This can often be mistaken for addiction. It's not as bad, but it's still not ideal.

Smartphones provide a lot of enjoyment. A social media 'like', a quick game, a fun app or selfie filter, a pleasant chat: all these provide a reliable and, more importantly, instant burst of pleasure, something your maturing brain is *incredibly* keen on, as we've seen before.

And a pleasure response **is enhanced by *novelty*.**

Something enjoyable? Great. Something enjoyable and *new*? Better! And smartphones, providing access to all information ever, plus a constant stream of real-time updates from friends and idols, offer *endless novelty*.

All that is hard to resist, especially in situations that *aren't* enjoyable (like a boring lesson, or a family gathering) where your brain's already working hard to stay focused. Simply having it within reach is a great temptation, like having someone endlessly whispering

PHONE! PHONE! PHONE! PHONE! PHONE!

into your ear.

That's why your smartphone *can* be disruptive, *particularly* at school.

You'd think it would be great for your education – always having a calculator, a translator, a map and an infinite library of information in your pocket.

But we saw how having your friends nearby, who you enjoy interacting with, can distract you from your lesson. Imagine how much more distracting it is to have *every single one* of your friends and the other people you like 'present' at all times! That's basically what a smartphone offers you.

Taking your smartphone to school usually just means forcing yourself to ignore the temptations it offers you. And those efforts could be better spent elsewhere. Like, on studying, which, although often dull, is still *essential*.[38]

So, you're not addicted to your phone, as your parents insist (or fear), but you could (and probably should) try to put it down and do literally anything else from time to time.

In early 2019, the Royal College of Paediatrics and Child Health, pretty much the go-to experts for this kind of thing, published up-to-date guidelines about the effects of 'screen time' (the catch-all term for the use of smartphones, tablets, video games, etc.) on the development of children and teenagers. In a nutshell, they said that there was *no evidence that screen time damages your brain or causes lasting harm*. However, they *do* advise moderation and control. So, pretty much the same as the advice for parents and drinking wine.

38. Indeed, some schools now have policies banning smartphones from lessons, and, in general, academic performance goes up while stress and anxiety go down. Just something to consider.

'IS USING MY PHONE UNHEALTHY?'

In themselves, smartphones are pretty much perfectly safe. They don't damage your health by beaming toxic signals directly into your eyeballs or anything weird like that.

It's just that, while smartphones provide stimulation for your brain, they provide very little stimulation for your body. They make you just sit there for long periods. And that *is* unhealthy.

Especially for teenagers.

Inactivity isn't something your body handles any better than your brain, particularly when it's flooded with stimulating hormones, and growing fast.

Moreover, not getting any sunlight (because you're always indoors, on your phone) means that your skin can't manufacture enough vitamin D, a vital hormone. Insufficient vitamin D during childhood and adolescence is linked to many long-lasting health problems.

There could be many good reasons for not getting regular exercise (injury, illness, disability, etc.), but 'too distracted by my phone' isn't one of them.

And constantly holding and looking down at a smartphone can damage your posture, as the nerves, joints and muscles in your neck and shoulders are overtaxed.

You need your neck and shoulders for lots of things, so this isn't good.

Some also report repetitive strain injury in the thumbs from persistent smartphone use. Or *visual* issues. Your eyes develop and change along with the rest of your body: constantly staring at something right in front of you tells your developing visual system that this near focus is all you need, so the ability to focus on things further away is impaired, meaning you might need glasses.

And then there are the injuries sustained when you're distracted by your phone and walk into traffic, or fall down a manhole!

Accidents like this don't happen nearly as often as people assume, but there have been several reported deaths of people who ventured into dangerous places to get a nice backdrop for a selfie.[39]

Your brain may enjoy all the activity smartphones provide, but your body needs activity too, along with exposure to the outdoors, or your health will suffer. And excessive smartphone use usually *deprives* you of these things.

So yeah, I'm sorry to say that your parents' concerns are mostly valid here.

39. I think we can all agree that 'death' is unhealthy, right?

'DOES MY SMARTPHONE DISRUPT MY SLEEP?'

Yes. We covered this in chapter two.

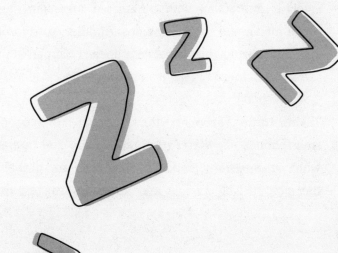

'IS USING MY PHONE UNSOCIABLE?'

Yes and no.

Your parents may see you absorbed in your phone, ignoring everyone around you, not going out and meeting people, just staring at a small glowing screen. What's sociable about that?

But what are you *doing* with your phone? It usually involves interacting with others via messaging and social media and sharing memes. Another word for all that? Socializing! Just because it doesn't happen in the same room doesn't mean it's not happening at all.

Taking into account the number of people smartphones allow you to communicate and interact with *simultaneously*, modern teenagers are probably the *most sociable humans ever*. Statistics suggest that communicating with others, *socializing*, is the main thing smartphones are used for!

So yeah – take that, parents!

However, it's not all good.

Face-to-face interaction is still an essential part of life.

You can't do *everything* online, because you're not a brain in a jar (yet).

And real-world interactions can make up in quality what they lack in quantity. There's a lot more going on with them; it's a much richer sensory experience than some text and a profile photo.

Remember, we're a social species; we've evolved to appreciate eye contact and facial expressions. You can see this in the workings of the brain.

However, the temptation to prioritize your phone over direct interaction with other people is strong. Sometimes *too* strong.

Say you're talking to someone, and you get a message alert on your phone. Do you answer it right away? A *lot* of people do.

But what you're doing here is interrupting the conversation you're having with a person *right in front of you* to respond to some *unknown* person *far away*. You're saying:

I DON'T KNOW WHO THIS DISTANT PERSON WHO WANTS MY ATTENTION IS, BUT THEY'RE MORE IMPORTANT TO ME THAN YOU AND THIS DISCUSSION.

That's unsociable, right?

In fact, it's rude.

The problem is, as with learning in school, being sociable is important, but it's not always enjoyable. Sometimes it's tedious. But it's still *essential* for forging strong relationships and developing communication skills, a vital part of life, particularly adult life.

Unfortunately, while smartphones enhance online socialization, they often get in the way of the real-world equivalent. They offer immediate novelty, and real-life conversations often don't. Your brain gets an instant reward from the icon of a sent message, or a 'like' or comment; in a more ambiguous conversation, the reward is much harder to assess.

So your teenage brain will often opt for the phone in your pocket over whoever's in front of you. This can have unpleasant social consequences.

Smartphones focus on 'fun' socialization. And life can't always be fun. Sorry.

'IS MY SMARTPHONE DAMAGING MY BRAIN?'

This is a bit of a grey area, but the claims that smartphones cause lasting harm to your brain are mostly unfounded. And often pretty irrational.

A few parents worry about 'sensory overload' – the fear that your devices provide too much stimulation for you to handle. But think about it: in the course of *every waking moment* your senses are bombarding your brain with a full-colour, high-resolution, 3D surround-sound experience, with smells, tastes and touch thrown in too.

Your brain seems to handle this just fine. A few hours spent watching images on a small screen is hardly going to burn it out, is it?

In fact, individuals with autism often prefer to use screens, because the information is way more organized than the chaos of everyday life. It's weird to think that a smartphone might provide *reduced* stimulation compared to the real world, but there you go.

'WHAT ABOUT MY MEMORY?'

More common, and arguably more reasonable, are claims that smartphones stunt or disrupt important cognitive abilities. Most importantly, your attention span and memory.

Many people even insist that smartphones cause *physical changes* in your brain that impair these abilities. Smartphones are *disrupting your brain's development*!

There is a logic to all this. After all, your brain *is* developing and maturing. And we've seen that it needs to experience certain things in order to become good at processing them.

But now, for the first time ever, young people have smartphones, which produce new and interesting things all the time, so their attention doesn't *stay* focused on any one thing. They don't have to pay attention or concentrate, so these abilities won't develop. That will surely damage their attention span!

Also, thanks to smartphones, young people have access to the internet, so they can look up any information they need. They never have to retain any facts, so they rarely use their memory! Obviously the memory doesn't develop in the right way!

The logic behind these concerns is pretty watertight, right?

Except, it's not.

When using a smartphone, aren't you're paying *more* attention to *multiple* things, rather than just staring at a boring newspaper, like your parents? So, rather than damaging your attention span, why wouldn't smartphones *improve* it, and enhance your ability to multitask?

Moreover, if you're constantly looking things up, aren't you taking in loads of new information? Aren't smartphones *making your memory work harder* than ever? Shouldn't they be boosting your memory system as a result?

These arguments are just as logical as the ones that cause parents to panic, yet they say the exact opposite. They can't *both* be right.

So, what does the actual scientific evidence say?

There's not really that much of it. There hasn't been enough *time* to study the long-term consequences of using smartphones. They're so new that the 'long term' hasn't happened yet!

ATTENTION SPAN

A few studies have shown that, if there's a smartphone next to them, people have a reduced ability to focus on a task. Like, say, being taught something at school?

The human brain has a limited attention capacity – you'll have experienced this if you've ever been made to do more than two things at once. Your parents may yell that you need to clean your room *now* while you're in the middle of homework, just as your brother or sister is trying to tell you something.

You quickly become 'overwhelmed', and probably yell at everyone to

Your brain cannot focus on and deal with multiple demands, and this has caused it to overload.

However, your attention system doesn't just hang around waiting for something to happen. If you know there's something that *might* happen, your brain, often via the threat-detection system we talked about earlier, diverts part of your attention to watch out for it, so it doesn't take you by surprise.

Even if it's not yours, a smartphone might ring, vibrate or start playing music at any second. Your ever-vigilant brain knows this, so it'll be preoccupied with it, just in case. Meaning you have a *reduced attention for other things*. So if a smartphone, any smartphone, is nearby, you'd expect it to reduce your attention and focus.

Imagine if you were made to do a task next to a chimp. Even if it was sitting quietly, you'd be *distracted* by it, wouldn't you? But people don't rant about chimps damaging your attention span!

That's probably because nobody carries a chimp in their pocket wherever they go!

Some studies show that people who admit to using smartphones excessively also do poorly in tests measuring attention and focus. Even when their phone is nowhere to be seen.

It's tempting to read this and conclude that smartphones *do* damage your attention span and ability to focus. But what if the study is actually showing that people who have limited attention spans and struggle to focus *check their smartphones more*? Because they would, wouldn't they? It's a chicken-and-egg situation: we don't know which comes first.

Other studies argue that smartphones and electronic devices limit your ability to recall information, suggesting they damage your memory. But a lot of it boils down to the fact that you're focusing *on your phone*. For instance, when you take a photo of something with your phone, most of your attention is directed at the phone. If you didn't have it, you'd be focusing on the thing you're taking a photo of; it would occupy your available brain space, making it easier to form lasting, detailed memories of it. Adding your phone into the process makes this harder.

When your parents urge you to stop videoing or photographing an event and just *enjoy* it – to 'live in the moment' – they probably have a point.

The few studies that *have* looked into the effect of smartphones on the brain *haven't found anything conclusive*. And for every study that shows that smartphones are damaging, there's one that shows they have no effect, or even a *good* effect.

Some studies have shown that playing first-person-shooter video games like *Halo* or *Call of Duty* seems to *increase* your cognitive abilities.

It makes sense – all the weapons changes and sniper shots and squad coordination and cover-based combat happening quickly and randomly – you clearly need some serious brain power just to keep up with that.

This discovery hasn't really caught on with parents, though. Funny, that.

Ultimately, even if we accept that smartphones and other devices can distract and preoccupy you, there's no evidence to show that they do *permanent damage* to the way your brain works. Smartphones do a lot of things, and this means you *don't have to make your brain do them*. But it doesn't mean that your brain *can't* do these things.

But the problem is, *we don't know for sure* what dangers smartphones pose. **It's too soon to say.**

This doesn't mean that they are 100 per cent guaranteed safe, and we've seen that there are risks from excessive use, particularly for a maturing brain like yours.

'WHAT ABOUT HOW I SOCIALIZE?'

There's one particular aspect of smartphone use that seems to cause a lot of concern.

Social media.

How many social networks are you part of? I'm nearly forty years old, so you're probably active on ones I've never even heard of, but I assume they all involve sharing updates and aspects of your life with other people, who do the same.

That's what social media is for, really. Sounds harmless, right?

Not necessarily. Many people worry about the effects of social media, particularly when it comes to teenagers. Indeed, recent evidence suggests that teenagers who spend a lot of time on social media are more likely to experience episodes of poor mental health.

How, though?

Good question.

For starters, it's yet another thing that can keep you awake with constant stimulation and novelty, and we know why that's bad.[40]

More importantly, though, it is linked to something we covered in the previous chapter: the desire to be accepted and liked by others. We saw how this can be a huge source of pressure, stress and uncertainty for younger people like you.

Well, social media seriously messes around with the parts of your brain responsible for all this. In some ways, this is really good. In others, it's really *bad*.

We want – we *need* – others to like us, and we've seen that our brains instinctively make us do whatever we can to present ourselves in a good light, right? But social media takes this to a whole other level.

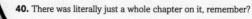

40. There was literally just a whole chapter on it, remember?

Social media gives you much greater control over how you appear. You can take hundreds of selfies and choose the best one before sharing, so you can look your best, with zero flaws or quirks. Acne, blemishes, unsightly bulges, wonky eyeliner – none of that is an issue online.

You can also spend time wording the perfect post or comment or reply; you don't have to do it in the moment and risk saying something stupid (like calling your mate Dan 'Dad', causing everyone to make fun of you forever).

Social media also provides easy access to *more people than ever*. You're not limited to four or five friends at once. Now you can interact with and gain the approval of *hundreds*, *thousands*, even *millions*, if your YouTuber career is going well.

And every friend request or follow, every share, 'like', nice comment, smiley emoji reply, these are demonstrations that people accept and *like* you.

Social media provides many more opportunities to be liked and accepted, with little of the risk or effort involved in face-to-face interactions.

Given that your teenage brain is desperate for approval and terrified of rejection, is it any wonder that social media is so tempting? It's like giving a hungry cat a giant vat of fresh cream.

But then, no matter how much the cat likes cream, if you drop it into a vat of the stuff, it could still drown.

You can have too much of a good thing. And that goes for social media.

AN UNREALISTIC VIEW

Social media can make bullying and harassment easier, for starters. We've seen why people are bullies, but when you can do it from a safe distance, with fewer chances of retaliation? It's very tempting for these people to make themselves feel better by trying to bring others down. That's how we get trolls.

Other dangers are less obvious.

Think about this: social media allows you to present yourself in the most positive way, to make people like and respect you. But *everyone else* is probably doing that as well! And remember, we figure out our own worth, our self-esteem, by comparing ourselves to others.

Social media provides **a seriously unrealistic view of others**.

With all the needs, pressures and stresses placed on you and your maturing brain, teenagers can, and regularly do, suffer from low self-esteem. And, for all the enjoyment and positivity it can provide, social media bombards you with images of other people who are happy, beautiful or successful. Or all three.

Or at least that's what they're *saying* they are. Particularly those Instagram influencers, who look like they live their lives in one long glamorous underwear advert.

Except, they're *not*. At least, not all the time. But you *only* see the good stuff. (Which is often exaggerated by filters, Photoshop, etc.)

Imagine if, when you did a test, your teachers only ever counted correct answers and ignored the wrong ones, so everyone got 100 per cent. The school reports would make it seem like your class was stuffed with super geniuses.

But it's *not*. Brian, who keeps accidentally gluing his head to the desk? Madeline, who genuinely thinks dolphins are fairy-tale creatures? These aren't super geniuses. To get a *real* idea of the situation, you need to know the negatives as well as the positives. The human brain already works hard to hide or downplay the negatives of our lives, but social media encourages this tendency.

Scrolling through feeds showing happy people and their brilliant lives and comparing them to your own unedited life can make you feel so much worse.

You only know about *your own* problems. You're living them from the inside. Nobody else seems to have any. Based on this (wrong) information, it's easy to conclude that you're flawed, inadequate. This can seriously damage self-esteem, worsen moods and increase stress, which we know can lead us to look at other people's feeds even more, and we know where *that* ends up.

Anxiety.
Mood disorders.
Depression.

And one symptom of depression is *focusing on why we're bad, flawed, unworthy*. It soon becomes self-sustaining.

That's how too much social media can harm your mental health.

GET ACTIVE

What happens if you put yourself out there, reach out and talk to people, become active and open up about what you're feeling? Evidence suggests that this helps with mental health issues. Sharing improves your own understanding of mental well-being, enhances your self-worth, gives a sense of community and belonging, and so much more. All of which can be beneficial.

These are small steps, but they can make all the difference. And if your parents see what you're doing, hopefully their concerns will be allayed and they won't mind so much when you *do* use your smartphone. They're only used to scare stories – maybe they'll even be interested in this side of the online world?

We've seen that social media can cause stress, but you may not *recognize* this. Social media is enjoyable, something you *choose* to do in a life where it seems you don't get many choices, so you're less likely to see it as a problem.

When your parents say things like 'You spend too much time on social media', they may have a point.
For once.

PARENTS VS PHONES

The available facts show us that smartphones are a mixed bag. The big picture is very uncertain.

Of course, none of this helps you avoid arguments if your parents still insist that smartphones are bad for you. And many parents do, even though there's little to back this up.

Why is this? One reason is that, once we've settled on an opinion or belief, we're often reluctant to change our mind.

That's just how our brains work. We've processed a lot of information to reach our conclusions; the brain is a very busy organ and doesn't like having to start all over again. That's why people have a habit of latching on to any information, or argument, that agrees with their views, and ignoring or denying things that say they're wrong.

When you argue with your parents because you feel totally differently about something, it seems you'll never agree! You both dig your heels in, refusing to back down.

This isn't weird; *everyone*'s brain does this (although some more than others). If you've ever argued with someone online, you'll know how frustrating it is.

Many parents are *already* wary of smartphones, so they tend to believe any argument that backs up this suspicion, *no matter how little actual evidence there is*. That's why claims about the dangers of smartphones are so widespread, despite very little proof.

But why are parents suspicious of smartphones and other devices in the first place?

At one point in history, adults (often with many children of their own) were angrily warning of the dangers posed by the *printing press*! Yes, *reading* was once considered harmful! How times change.

When I was younger, there were media meltdowns over the dangers of video games:

they were apparently causing children and teens to crave violence!

And remember, back then video games looked like blocky cartoons. What would those outraged reporters have thought of today's ultra-realistic shooters, with authentic blood splatter and fifty different sounds of bones shattering? As we've got used to computer games being part of the world, the focus has moved on to social media.[41]

In general, parents seem to be suspicious of any new technology. Right now it's even worse because we're at a unique time in history, one which probably won't happen again (although you never know).

---

41. It could be the case that many of the adults making these claims about social media were the same kids who played video games growing up, and don't see anything wrong with *them*. But social media? That's unnatural!

DIGITAL NATIVES AND DIGITAL IMMIGRANTS

At the time of publication in 2019, we have a generation of *digital natives* being raised by a generation of *digital immigrants*.

What does that mean?

When your parents were growing up, *there was no internet*.

The internet wasn't just another technical convenience, like a slightly better iPhone; it changed how the world works!

And your parents saw it arrive. The world wasn't

online, 'digital', when they were born, but now it is. They *migrated* from one to the other. They're digital *immigrants*. They've arrived as adults, in a new world, not really speaking the language, picking up enough to get by but always feeling slightly like they're learning the rules as they go along.

You, though, were *born* into this digital world. You're *native* to it. A digital native. You grew up doing that finger-and-thumb thing to make an image get bigger on a screen. You knew your way around a smartphone pretty much from toddlerhood.

Remember, during childhood and your teens, your brain is at its most flexible and adaptable, and is good at dealing with change. For your parents, however, the internet (and smartphones, currently the main way of accessing it) appeared when their brains were done developing and maturing.

They didn't have enough flexibility to adapt, to accommodate this new reality.

Obviously, parents *can* learn all about the latest technical developments. Their brains still have a lot of give; it's not like trying to change the ingredients of a cake after you've baked it. Countless adults learned to love and embrace the online revolution.

But even then, there's probably still a part of them, stemming from their childhood understanding of what's normal, which will remain forever wary of new and unfamiliar modern tech.

For today's teenagers, saying that you had no internet growing up is like saying you lived in an era before trees were invented. It's baffling: trees have always been there. And so has the internet and all that goes with it.

This highlights the differences between you and your parents in your approach to smartphones and related technology.

When your parents try to talk to you about technology, it's like they're using a language they're still learning, while you're fluent. If you regularly drop words into conversation like 'meme', 'gif', 'lol', 'roflcopter', 'PewDiePie', 'BFFs' and so on, they'll look at you blankly.[42]

---

42. Yes, I did have to look many of those up. On the internet, ironically.

Some parents will try to keep up and communicate on your level, even though they aren't quite . . . capable of it. I was in a supermarket once and overheard a mother say to her teenage son:

CHICKEN NUGGETS.
HASHTAG COOL, YEAH?

I don't know what happened next – I was too busy cringing.

This difference in attitudes towards technology can lead to friction and further arguments, especially if it upsets the parent–child relationship.

Your parents are older, more experienced, wiser, while you're still learning and developing. The power balance in your relationship should reflect this. *They* should be in charge.

But, as we've seen, modern technology and online culture are areas where you often *know more* than your parents. Imagine trying to maintain authority over an argumentative teenager when you also need to ask them how to reset the Wi-Fi router, or how to upload a picture to Facebook!

When you're out and about in the real world, parents can find out where you are, what you're doing, who you're with, and can help out if you get into trouble.[43]

However, most parents *can't* do that when it comes to your online habits. You could be talking to a shifty forty-five-year-old hiding behind the profile of a twelve-year-old girl, or being persuaded to join a cult, and they'd never know; they couldn't do much about it if they did, because you know your way around the online world better than they do.

No parent likes this. Is it any wonder that they are suspicious of phones and devices? For you, these are just another (very useful and enjoyable) part of the world. It doesn't make sense to be angry at a smartphone, any more than it does to be angry at a bus stop. But your parents see them as a new thing that damages their relationship with their child. To make things worse, they can't even compare their experience to that of their parents when *they* were young – because there weren't any smartphones then.

---

43. This is why many parents *like* you to have a smartphone.

This situation isn't great for you either.

You're already predisposed to resent authority and loss of independence, so having your parents lecture you about your phone use even though they don't know nearly as much as you do about how it all works? That's seriously aggravating.

And your phone isn't just some annoying gadget; it's your link to all your friends and the wider world (which your parents and society prevent you from exploring for real). Why *should* you have to surrender that because of their unfounded fears?

'YOUR PHONE IS DANGEROUS. MINE IS FASCINATING.'

What about parents who don't follow these rules *themselves*. Who criticize you for using your phone instead of interacting with your family while they're constantly playing around with theirs? They may say that it's OK when they do it because it's 'work', or give some other excuse!

Why should that make a difference? You might ask if using your phone is dangerous and rude; it shouldn't matter *why* you're using it! You eat a bucket of rotten mince, you'll be violently sick, whether it was for a dare from mates or because your boss told you to.

But then maybe smartphones *are* more dangerous for your maturing brain than they are for your parents' more rigid ones? There's no concrete evidence for this yet, but we can't rule it out.

One thing we *can* say, though, is that both parents and teenagers go too far. Teenagers tend to ignore the downsides and hazards of smartphone use, while parents go on about the risks and dangers, even if they themselves shamelessly enjoy the benefits of smartphones.

Two wrongs don't make a right. In this case, they make for constant arguments.

It's weird to think that, unless the internet goes away or is replaced by something different (which seems unlikely), this situation won't happen again. If you have children of your own, you'll be a lot more knowledgeable about what goes on online, and better able to relate to them.

You'll probably still argue with them just as much. You might end up sounding like a modern version of your own parents, yelling stuff like:

WHEN I WAS YOUR AGE, I ONLY HAD 500 INSTAGRAM FOLLOWERS, AND I WAS HAPPY WITH THAT!

Of course, by then Instagram may seem as quaint and old-fashioned as steam trains and record players, and your own children may laugh at you for even mentioning it. That's progress for you, though.

TROUBLESHOOTING

THE PROBLEM: Your parents keep giving you a hard time about using your smartphone too much. But your phone is a lifeline for you, and you often use it because it's easier than dealing with your parents. This leads to disputes and arguments.

THE CONSEQUENCES: Arguing about it can make things worse for everyone. There's probably enough conflict going on as it is, and escaping into your phone and the online world is your way of avoiding it. Arguing *about* your phone usage can mean that you use it *more* in defiance, retaliation, or to retain a sense of independence.

But this brings with it a number of health risks that shouldn't be ignored.

THE SOLUTIONS

1 **The first thing you should do is** ask yourself if you really do use your smartphone too much. Or if you use it a reasonable amount *but don't do anything else*.

2 **Try leaving the house for a few hours without your phone and see what happens.** Do you get frustrated, panicky, twitchy, irritable? This is a good sign that you're a bit *too* reliant on it.

3 **You can make it easier by not taking your phone everywhere**, or putting it out of reach so you're not compelled to check it all the time, or turning off the notifications, so it's not constantly demanding your attention.

4 **And if you are struggling to cut back on social media** evidence suggests that active use of social media can be *helpful*.

5 **It might be a good idea to ask your parents to *join you* in managing your smartphone use**, assuming they have a smartphone too. If they insist you don't bring yours to the dinner table, ask them to agree to the same rule. Or suggest that you *both* leave your phones behind next time you go out somewhere, and see what they say.

If they agree, great. If they *don't*, then you've some ammunition next time they give you grief about your smartphone use. Might be helpful?

After all, it's entirely possible for your parents to be the ones who are wrong . . .

CHAPTER 6

'YOU'LL UNDERSTAND WHEN YOU'RE OLDER!'

>>>**FAULT:** Parents seem to think they know best about every issue, when their information is almost always out of date.

As we near the end of this book, it's worth noting something important. It may be hard to accept, but when your parents try to stop you doing something they may be *right* to do so. It isn't always an error.

We now know that your teenage brain is good at many things, but thinking logically and calmly about the consequences of your decisions . . . isn't really one of them. You clearly *can* do it, because you do it all the time. It's just more *effort* for you, compared to adults.

Your emotions and impulses often prove overwhelming, meaning that you lash out, or do things you shouldn't, and usually wouldn't – like experimenting with alcohol and drugs.

Statistics show that young people are much more likely to be involved in car accidents (when they're driving) and violent crime, because you need a cool head in intense situations – and that's not something teenagers are known for!

This is where your controlling parents are useful: they can stop you getting into dangerous situations, *if you listen to them*. Which, unfortunately, your teenage brain is reluctant to do.

This is also why many parents become preoccupied with your sex life as you get older.

Let's be blunt: it's *always massively awkward* to talk about sex with your parents. However, they don't like talking about it any more than you do! You're their *child*! Do you think they *want* to picture you getting up to that sort of thing, any more than you want to picture them doing it?

But they *make the effort anyway*, no matter how unsettling (for both of you). The human sex drive is incredibly powerful, especially during your teenage years when you're flooded with hormones. Your parents have been through this, they'll know you really *want* to experience it, but have no useful knowledge.[44] And sex involves many risks and hazards (unwanted pregnancy, illnesses, even injuries resulting from inexperience and so on).

---

44. This is one area where looking it up online isn't that helpful. It usually leads to pornography. But pornography is to actual sex what Instagram is to everyday life: there's only a vague resemblance, and treating it as normal can cause problems in the real world.

Your parents want to spare you all that, so they try to share their wisdom, even if it makes everyone wish they could be hit by a meteor, just to end the embarrassment.

The thing is, your parents have adult brains, ones that have done all the necessary maturing, so they're better at recognizing the downsides and hazards of the things that seem so enticing to you. This is especially true when it comes to your safety and well-being, which is their main priority.

They're also older and more experienced. They've learned more; they know better how things work.

That's why you should always listen to your parents; thanks to their calm, sensible brains, what they think is always right.

However, there's a problem with this conclusion.

It's nonsense!

Sure, your parents might be right about a *lot* of things, but . . . *always* right?
No way!

Remember, your parents' attempts to fix your sleep patterns mess them up completely. Their efforts to get involved with your schoolwork backfire. They certainly don't know more than you do about online culture, but they lecture you about it anyway! And as for your mental health? Well . . .

It's good that your parents want to share their wisdom with you, but . . . what if this wisdom is *wrong*?

Because it often is. And if there's one particular theme running through everything we've covered so far, it's that your parents' understanding of certain things is generally . . .

PARENTS

out
of
date.

TEENAGERS

THINK ABOUT IT

- **You're not a small child any more**, but they still get frustrated when you don't act like one.

- **They're needlessly suspicious about smartphones and the internet**, even though these things are a major part of modern life.

- **They mock and dismiss the idea of being a YouTuber** but are fine with equally 'frivolous' things from their own youth.

- **They condemn your favourite music as 'rubbish'**, even though the music they like is dreary, tedious noise.

It's like there's a time difference between what's going on in your head, and what's going on in your parents'. Important stuff like sexuality, gender, mental health, politics and more – your parents' views and grasp of things often seem years, maybe even *decades*, behind the times.

And they seem to want to *keep it* this way, as if they're putting their fingers in their ears and singing

if you try to talk them round to your more modern take on important matters.

Unfortunately, it seems that adult brains can be very stubborn when it comes to accepting that things might have changed, like someone insisting that their hot-air balloon is quicker than your helicopter.

Your parents may do illogical things, like talking about their own youth as some sort of golden age, a time when 'everything made sense', instead of the dreary era of ridiculous haircuts, zero Wi-Fi, four TV channels and terrible coffee.

However, perhaps the biggest issue is this. You're a teenager, you're developing your understanding of how things work. But your parents are still a big part of your life, so a lot of that development *will be influenced by them*.

This is mostly fine. Essential, even. But by giving you the benefit of their wisdom, your parents risk passing their outdated views and ideas *on to you*! So *you* end up believing and embracing views and ideas that don't match how things really are. This can cause serious problems.

That's why it's not necessarily a bad thing when you disagree with your parents. You're often *right* to. It's just that, thanks to how their brains work, most adults will resist accepting this. If you pick them up on things they're wrong about, many parents fall back on the old excuse:

So, *why* is so much of what you'll apparently understand 'when you're older' *wrong*?

'WERE THINGS REALLY BETTER WHEN MY PARENTS WERE YOUNGER?'

Let's look at one of the more persistent (and annoying) habits of parents, and adults in general: insisting that things were better in their day. As well as being irritating and patronizing, it influences their behaviour towards you in many unhelpful ways.

Many assume that this is simply a result of getting old. *Of course* things seemed better when you were younger, because *you were younger*! You didn't have any of the stresses or aches or baldness or weight gain that come with age, so *obviously* you'll think more fondly of a time when you were in your prime. It's the whole 'school days are the best days of your life' claim all over again.

However, evidence suggests a cause that goes much deeper than grumbling about the effects of age on your body.

It seems that most adults do remember their own childhood and teenage years as being better than the present day.

But that's because **their memory is wrong!**

WHAT?!

This might sound a bit far-fetched. Sure, we've all remembered a name or an address wrong, or mixed up which actor was in which film. Nobody thinks memory is 100 per cent reliable. But how can the memory of *the first two decades of your life* be wrong?

Easily, as it happens.

In the last two chapters, we looked at how our brain boosts our self-esteem and makes us seem better, more likeable, by shaping our words and actions, to emphasize our good points and downplay the bad.

Bizarrely, this happens with our *memories* too.

It's been shown countless times: people remembering doing well on a test when they didn't, remembering they made a smart decision when they'd just flipped a coin, remembering being a key player in a match their football team won even though all they did was run around wheezing.

Nobody's *lying* here; they genuinely remember things happening that way.

Except, things *didn't* happen that way.

What happens is, your brain *alters* your memories, tweaks and adjusts them to exaggerate your performance.

When we remember being successful, **we feel better about ourselves**.

There's a limit to this, obviously. You can't honestly remember scoring the winning goal when your team lost, and you weren't even *there*. But if your brain can get away with tweaking memories, it will usually do just that.

Moreover, *good* memories outlast *bad* ones, in terms of how they affect us. When you think about a happy memory, you *feel* happy, right, while remembering something unfair makes you angry. Or a sad memory makes you . . . sad.

It makes sense: a memory of an emotional event *includes* the emotions you experienced, and you'll experience them again when remembering that event.

You meet someone with red hair, you'll see them with red hair whenever you remember them.

And, as we saw earlier, emotions are important to memory. Your brain doesn't arrange memories according to whether they contain useful information, no matter how helpful that would be. Instead, your brain logs memories with the most stimulating and/or *emotional* content as most important.

Getting your first bike, your first kiss, the time you nearly drowned in a pool, the death of your first pet: bad or good, these are all incredibly emotional experiences, ones you tend to remember your whole life.

The general rule is, the further back in your life you try to remember, the fewer memories you can recall. A few days or weeks ago? Fine. But several years ago? It's much harder to remember any specific details.

This *should* mean that, for adults, memories of childhood are mostly hazy, or forgotten. But they're *not*. Most adults remember their childhood and teenage years *better* than later points in their lives.

Scientists call this the '**reminiscence bump**'.

Why? Well, our brains label emotional memories as most important. And what are you always dealing with during your teens? *Very powerful emotions!* They might be a pain, but they do wonders for your memory.

However, there are limits to this, because the emotional element of memories gradually dwindles.

It's a bit like chewing gum: it's all minty freshness when you put it in your mouth, but eventually that fades, and you just have this bland lump. Similarly, your *memory* doesn't go away, but the emotional flavour, while it might never *completely* vanish, dissipates over time.

Interestingly, it seems that bad emotional memories fade *faster* than good ones. You can chew the gum of good memories for longer, and the flavour keeps coming.

Whatever the reasons for this, it means that older memories tend to be happier, more positive, than more recent ones, because the negative stuff has diminished with time.

Add all this up, and it means that your parents remember their childhood and teenage years *better* than most of their adult lives, but these memories *tend to be happy, positive ones*!

But remember, we've seen instances where only focusing on the positives and ignoring the negatives can have unpleasant results; for example, social media can ruin your self-esteem. And it's the same with thinking only good things about your childhood.

Many parents complain that kids today don't play outside enough, because they're always indoors with their smartphones and other devices. There are even *memes* about this![45]

Apparently, when they were young, parents regularly played outside, while you modern lazy kids stay indoors with your devices. And your parents are all the better for it.

Let's be clear:
this is absolute guff.

Did your parents choose playing outside over using devices because they had self-discipline and a healthy attitude? No, they didn't use smartphones because *they hadn't been invented yet*! If they had, your parents would have been *just as hooked on them*.

You don't get to act superior for avoiding something *that didn't exist*! It's like demanding a medal for not eating a cake that nobody has baked yet.

This super-positive warping of childhood memories means that adults can remember something that was

---

45. Yes, memes criticizing kids for spending too much time online, regularly posted by parents online. Is anyone else seeing a problem here?

the result of timing and luck, and honestly think it's a genuine *achievement*.

It also explains the 'school days are the best days of your life' thing, and why they don't seem to recognize how hard you are finding your teens, even though they surely *experienced the same thing*. Their brain has taken the memories of those times, Photoshopped all the flaws, fixed the lighting, slapped on several filters and said:

> YEP, THAT'S DEFINITELY WHAT IT WAS LIKE.

This also explains the differing musical tastes of different generations. Studies show that the music you experience during your teenage years is usually the music you'll prefer *for the rest of your life*!

It makes perfect sense. Music has many powerful effects on your brain: it's stimulating, rich and rewarding, and can produce *strong emotions*! The teenage brain is hugely receptive to music, so the music of your youth will resonate with you forever, while anything that comes later (or before, in many cases) won't have the same effect. It *can't*. And so you get people of different ages constantly bickering about what proper music is.

There's a good chance there was nothing particularly special about the music of your parents' youth. It's more that *they* were special. They were teenagers. Like you.

Things weren't better when your parents were younger, but their brains have made the *memories* of those times more rosy than they should be. So, if they complain about how you live your life because their childhood was superior? That's like accusing someone of being overweight because you had a *dream* where they were thinner.

This tendency also means that adults may place more value on experiences and information obtained during that time, and rely on them way more than they should. And that's not great.

'SHOULD I ALWAYS RESPECT THE OPINIONS OF MY ELDERS?'

Here's something infuriating that happens a lot when you're young.

Say you disagree with a parent (or any adult) over something. Doesn't matter what. You might think it makes perfect sense for billionaires to use their money to make sure very poor people can eat, rather than using it to buy a thirteenth gold yacht. Or it might be that you think someone at school should be allowed to decide whether they want to be referred to as 'she' or 'he'. Or that we should try to look after the only planet we have. Whatever.

Your parents don't agree. But rather than trying to persuade you that they're right with reason and logic, they just point out that they're older than you, which apparently makes them automatically correct.

If they're nice about it, they'll use the classic 'you'll understand when you're older' response. So, unless they want to pick up the argument again in twenty years when you *are* older, there's nothing you can do about it.

Or they can be a bit more aggressive, and insist that you 'respect your elders', because you're young and don't know anything, and should 'know your place'.

Again, this is mostly wrong.

Nobody automatically knows more because they've been alive longer. Your brain doesn't just absorb information from the air; **you *work* for it**.

You can take a book out of the library for a month and never read it, while someone else can take it out for a week and read it from cover to cover. Who's had the book longer? But who knows more about it?

Unfortunately, many adults cling to their misinformed opinions rather firmly. It's as if an opinion gets 'righter' with age.[46]

We've already looked at this in chapter five, where we saw how the human brain is generally *very resistant to being wrong*, to changing its (*our*) mind, meaning we tend to believe anything that agrees with us (no matter how ridiculous) but doubt anything that disagrees (no matter how sensible).

When presented with an argument or idea in which we can't see any obvious flaw, we look for other reasons to undermine it. Say the person disagreeing with you is young, therefore you think, *They must be wrong in some way, right? They're not old enough to know more than me. So, I can reject their ideas.*

This is called the 'ad hominem' fallacy, if you want to be posh about it. In simpler terms, you know the phrase 'play the ball, not the man'? This is the opposite of that.

---

46. Which it doesn't.

Someone says, 'I can't explain why your argument is wrong, but it must be because you're the "wrong" sort of person.'

Do parents do this? Maybe, but not so aggressively and so blatantly, and not necessarily deliberately. A lot of this stuff happens in the lower regions of your thinking, where you're not aware of it.

Sometimes it's just a time-saving thing. Parents often lack the energy or patience to get into a long, detailed discussion, so they might just use being older as a get-out excuse to end the argument quickly.

Whatever the reasons behind it, it means that parents are unlikely to shift from their existing views and opinions, even when (or especially when) they clash with yours.

This sticking-to-your-guns approach causes a lot of problems. Adults acquired most of their understanding during their childhood and teenage years. But the world has *moved on* since then; things have advanced, new information is being made available all the time.

So, you get adults (the ones with all the power and control) clinging to ideas and views that are **decades out of date**.

This doesn't apply to teenagers: your flexible brain is still working things out, so you take the latest ideas and discoveries in your stride. If anything, your instinctive dislike of anything safe and familiar means you're more drawn to things your parents don't like or disagree with.

Naturally, this leads to arguments.

Take sexuality. Many modern adults are OK with, or at least *aware of*, people being homosexual or bisexual. But what about people being polyamorous? Or asexual? Or pansexual?

Younger people usually have little trouble under-standing, or embracing, these concepts. But many adults remain perplexed by these more 'recent' additions to the sexuality spectrum.[47] Older adults probably grew up in a far more heteronormative environment (meaning they were told that men liked women, women liked men, and that was it). Anything different to that was wrong, in some way. And to many people, *it still is.*

Are they older? Yes. Are they *right*? No.

This also applies to gender fluidity: the right to define your own gender identity as something beyond or alternative to what your anatomy dictates is an extremely hot-button topic lately, but younger people tend to be more OK with it.

Or economics: media articles complain that young people aren't buying enough cars or houses or other luxury goods, while younger people point out that they can't afford any of these things because of suppressed wages and student loans.[48]

---

47. Many people will point out that they're not 'recent'; they've *always* been there, and it's just we're allowed to talk about them now.

48. Things the older generations (who write these whining articles) never had to deal with, interestingly.

There are many things older and younger generations disagree on – often because adults stick to principles and ideas that, while normal in their youth, are now largely obsolete, at least as far as younger people's lives are concerned.

Sadly, this means that outdated, even harmful ideas can last way longer than they should. As I said earlier, if our understanding and beliefs about how things work are built up during childhood and our teen years, much of them will be shaped by our parents.

For example, if your parents believed that all dogs were dangerous, they would definitely tell you that, and they'd keep you away from dogs, so you'd never get the chance to learn otherwise. You'd grow up convinced that all dogs were dangerous.
Because, how could you not?

Even though *most dogs are not dangerous.*

It's easy to see how ideas can be passed down from generation to generation. *Whether they're right or not!*

This can be very bad.

'CAN SO MANY ADULTS POSSIBLY BE WRONG?'

A lot of the notions your parents have about how things work are very common, and held by millions of others. That's great.

But just because ideas are widely held and well established, that doesn't mean they're *right*. For decades, people thought slavery, women being unable to vote, smoking, fossil fuels and petrol cars were fine and dandy. But now, in the modern day, we see that wasn't the case.

And there are many other things widely accepted by adults that are *harmful* to you, and you'd be absolutely *right* to challenge them!

For instance, teenage girls experience more mental health problems than teenage boys, and this is partly because of the expectations and pressure that they have to endure.

Young women are told that they *have to* be beautiful, slim and perfect *at the very least*, otherwise they're a failure.

How many TV shows, movies, magazines, adverts, social networks are stuffed with images of flawlessly beautiful women, with no blemishes or trace of body fat?

The fact that many of these rich and famous women have armies of stylists and make-up artists and personal trainers dedicated to making them look great is never mentioned. And their images are *still* enhanced via Photoshop to an impossible standard of beauty.

These images are presented as normal. You're *expected* to look like this. But the vast majority of young women can never hope to live up these standards, because they're *not real*. The result is that young women feel like failures just for existing in the form they're born with.

Their behaviour is put under a magnifying glass as well. They're told to be confident, but get criticized for being bossy. They're pressured to look sexy 24/7, but are also condemned for being 'cheap' or 'trashy'. And so on. They can't win.

Imagine an Olympic athlete who runs a mile in three minutes. That's an incredible achievement. However, instead of being rewarded and congratulated, from then on, they and every other runner are mocked and insulted whenever they *don't* run that fast.

That's how modern society often treats young women. And when we consider how self-esteem, acceptance and stress are key parts of mental health, is it any *wonder* teenage girls have difficulties with theirs?

Where do these pressures and expectations *come from*? They're not natural – they couldn't possibly be. No, they come from the world around us. The one shaped and controlled by adults. Like your parents.

I'm not saying that your parents are doing anything *on purpose*. Far from it. The same pressures were applied to them growing up. But this often means they internalize these ideas; they become part of their understanding of how the world works. And if countless other adults around them see things in the same way, why would they think to question them?

And so adults inadvertently communicate the same impossible pressures and ideals to girls, from a very early age.

Young girls are bombarded by princesses – they see princess toys, books and films. They're even *called* 'Princess'. **As a result, they want to *be* princesses.**

But what is this idea of a princess? A girl who has everything but didn't have to work for it?

And how do you become a princess? Unless you marry a prince (hugely unlikely), you have to be born one. So, any girl who isn't really a princess is *already a failure*! Is it any wonder that girls struggle with self-esteem?

Meanwhile, young men have a hard time of it too. They're just exposed to different expectations, with different consequences. Young men are under tremendous social pressure to be 'masculine'; the wider world expects them to be 'tough', 'strong', 'manly' and all that.

But being strong doesn't just mean 'able to lift heavy things'. Now it apparently means *not showing emotions*. Don't cry, don't be sad, don't get upset, don't be passionate about anything, don't hug, don't show any weakness or sensitivity. That's 'girly'.

However, men are also affected by issues of self-esteem, acceptance and stress. That's why this insistence that young men be strong, dominant, confident and *nothing else*, can be seriously damaging. Because you *can't be all those things all the time*.

Remember the athlete who *always* has to run a mile in three minutes?

For a man to show emotion and vulnerability, when everyone thinks he shouldn't, and he wants to be accepted? That takes *serious strength*. It's weird how few people recognize that.

Men are *just as emotional* as women, in terms of how their brains work. Unfortunately, anger is usually the only emotion men are allowed to express: one that often leads to conflict and fighting. 'Manly' things.

Remember, suppressing or denying your emotions is bad for your mental health, and not seeking help can lead to more harmful, dangerous options for dealing with it.

So, these ideas of what is 'manly' can damage teenage men's mental health.

According to the evidence, young women experience higher rates of mental health problems – possibly because they have *even more* impossible expectations to live up to. However, if you believe that showing vulnerability makes you less of a man, you probably wouldn't admit to mental health issues. You might even deny the possibility *to yourself.*

But *denying* them *doesn't* mean they aren't there! The fact that suicide is the biggest killer of men under thirty in the UK suggests they're struggling a lot more than they're willing, or able, to admit. And the ludicrous expectations of what it means to be 'manly' *stop them from seeking vital help* when they need it most.

Again, where do these expectations come from? Mostly, adult society, which includes your parents.

If you create a world where the phrase 'man up!' is used to mean 'stop showing any emotion of any sort!' **that will have consequences**.

We *know* that these expectations, and views on how men and women should act and think, are wrong, unrealistic, often impossible and harmful. And yet they're as common as they've ever been!

These ideals, along with many others, are maintained (and passed on) by adults and their more-rigid brains. They're not guilty of doing anything deliberately wrong; these are just the ideals they were brought up with. So, they inform their understanding of how the world and everyone in it *should* be.

It's already hard enough for adults, but being a parent can make you even *less* likely to change your mind, your understanding. You need to provide structure, order, guidance for your child. It's hard to do that if you're constantly rethinking everything you know. And if you get things wrong it could *harm your child*.

However well meant, this can mean that your parents accidentally make life *harder* for you.

Say they want to protect you from a 'poor' decision, like being a YouTuber, because they see it as a pointless, childish, even embarrassing pursuit and don't want you to waste time or face disappointment. So, they criticize, even mock, the whole idea, which makes you feel bad about your enthusiasm.

It never occurs to them that their idea of being a YouTuber is woefully old-fashioned. Or that watching meaningless nonsense on TV was totally fine when they were your age. That totally passes them by.

While most of the things your parents believe are valid, resulting from years of experience, they can be absolutely certain they're right, and still be wrong.

That's another reason why your teens are such an important time. We know you're driven to seek independence, mostly from your parents. But this can also mean independence from your parents' *expectations and certainties.*

You're more likely to be drawn to the new and unfamiliar, and want **to avoid the stale and familiar**.

This means you're likely to reject your parents' views or expectations. This can be distressing for them, sure, but if their ideas are outdated, incorrect or harmful, then it's *good* to reject them.

Adults like your parents struggle to change their understanding, but they also make all the decisions about how the world works, so these unhelpful and harmful views persist. If you manage to break free of them during your teenage years, when you have the drive and flexibility to do so, you could bring about changes when *you're* the adult.

It could be that you teenagers are the ones who **change the world for the better**.

Wouldn't be the first time.

TROUBLESHOOTING

THE PROBLEM: **You disagree with your parents about important, even fundamental, things.** They insist they're right because they're wiser, older, more experienced, all that. But their understanding of things is out of date, though it's really hard to tell them that. And they may even pass these (mis)understandings on to you.

THE CONSEQUENCES: **Disagreeing with your parents is never ideal**, but avoiding arguments by accepting their (wrong) views and fulfilling their expectations can be harmful to you. Your well-being may also suffer as you try to conform to ideals and expectations you don't like or agree with, which can be very stressful.

Letting your parents' incorrect views go unchallenged also means they are less likely to change them, although making *that* happen is hard.

THE SOLUTIONS

1 **If you and your parents are unable to agree on something**, for whatever reason, don't dwell on that one specific topic or issue; instead, mix it up a bit.

For instance, if you argue with your parents about what you're allowed to wear, it could help to bring up something related that you *do* agree on.

Maybe you can't agree on what's acceptable for someone your age, but you *can* agree that a certain relative's outfit at a family event was ridiculous. Or you can agree on something you wore that was liked by all, and work from there.

2 **When parents and teenagers argue about seemingly incompatible views**, it helps to show versatility.

The ability to express a *wide range* of emotions during disagreements (not just anger and resentment) shows that you have a strong, healthy relationship. Sure, your parents may be blatantly *wrong* about something, but that has less impact if you can regard it as *one* thing you don't agree on, among many things on which you *do*.

It can be *hard* to get away from the focus of an argument, especially when you're angry or upset, but it's often worth the effort. It might be something you'll have to come back to later, but if your parents are *particularly* wrong, and stubborn about it, then you'll definitely have your chance to do that.

ONE
LAST
THING

When you were a child, your parents were the masters of your universe, who knew everything and could do anything. But now you're a teenager you realize that's not what they are. It can be quite a revelation, and it means that your relationship is constantly being renegotiated.

Remember, although they once seemed all-knowing and all-powerful, your parents aren't that. They're just people.

People with flawed and quirky brains that often make things harder than they need to be.

People who want to be liked, to be successful.

People who care for those who matter to them.

People who deal with the constant stresses and hassle life throws at them every day.

People who have flaws and problems, and who deal with them as best they can.

People who probably went through the exact same things with *their* parents.

People . . .

. . . just like YOU.

A NOTE FROM THE AUTHOR

A big reason why I wanted to write this book was to try to help young people find a common ground with their parents and carers. But I also know that sometimes we all need someone else to talk to.

Anyone thinking that they might have a mental health problem should speak to their GP or a similarly registered professional before attempting to address matters by themselves.

However, I hope that the sources provided below can help guide you to better understand what's happening.

Childline

www.childline.org.uk

A free, private and confidential service for young people under the age of 19, where you can talk about anything, whatever your worry, whenever you need help.

Call: 0800 1111

Health for Teens

www.healthforteens.co.uk

An online resource created by the NHS to deliver guidance and support for struggling young people aged 11–19. They cover concerns from physical, mental and sexual health to societal pressures and lifestyle changes. They also run a ChatHealth service where young people are able to contact their local public health nursing team 24/7 via text message. Go to www.healthforteens.co.uk/health/about-chathealth for more information about the ChatHealth texting service in your local area.

NSPCC

www.nspcc.org.uk

The leading children's charity in the UK, specializing in child protection and dedicated to the fight for every childhood. Their specialists are available 24/7, 365 days a year.

Adults helpline: 0808 800 5000
Children and young people helpline –
Call Childline: 0800 1111

Young Minds

www.youngminds.org.uk

A leading charity that fights for children and young people's mental health. They offer information and guidance to enlighten and support those suffering from mental health issues.

Parents helpline (free; weekdays 9.30 a.m.–4 p.m.):
0808 802 5544
YoungMinds Crisis Messenger (free; 24/7): Text 'YM'
to 85258

Action on Addiction

www.actiononaddiction.org.uk

A national charity that offers high-quality, effective residential rehab and community-based addiction treatment.

Call: 01747 832 070

Addaction

www.addaction.org.uk

Addaction is one of the UK's largest drug and alcohol treatment and mental health charities helping addicts and their families deal with the effects of drug and alcohol misuse. As well as adult services, they also provide services specially tailored to the needs of young people and parents.

Webchat: www.addaction.org.uk/webchat
(weekdays 10 a.m.–4 p.m., 6 p.m.–9 p.m.;
weekends 11 a.m.–4 p.m.)

CALM
(Campaign Against Living Miserably)

www.thecalmzone.net

Leading a movement against male suicide by supporting men who are down or in crisis, and supporting those bereaved by suicide. Their 365-day helpline for men over 15 years old is open from 5 p.m. to midnight..

Call: 0800 58 58 58

Family Lives

www.familylives.org.uk

A national charity that specializes in professional, non-judgemental support and advice for families. Nearly all their services are free and they can be contacted 365 days a year.

Call: 0808 800 2222

Frank

www.talktofrank.com

The national drugs charity that provides comprehensive information about drugs and offers free confidential support and advice 24/7, 365 days a year.

Call: 0300 123 6600
Text: 82111

Mind

www.mind.org.uk

A mental health charity that aims to empower anyone experiencing a mental health problem by providing advice and support, to make sure that no one has to face these problems alone.

Mind Infoline (weekdays 9 a.m.–6 p.m.): 0300 123 3393
Text: 86463

Papyrus

www.papyrus-uk.org

The national charity working to give hope to young people under the age of 35 and to prevent young suicide. They provide confidential support and advice to vulnerable young people or those concerned about their loved ones.

HopelineUK: 0800 068 41 41
(weekdays 10 a.m.–10 p.m.; weekends 2 p.m.–10 p.m.)

Relate

www.relate.org.uk

The UK's largest provider of relationship support for all ages, backgrounds, sexual orientations and gender identities to strengthen their relationships. To find help in your area visit www.relate.org.uk/find-your-nearest-relate.

Telephone or webcam counselling booking line:
0300 003 0396

Samaritans

www.samaritans.org

The organization that offers a totally anonymous, non-religious and confidential crisis line to provide non-judgemental, emotional support to anyone feeling down or desperate. Available for free 24/7, 365 days a year.

Call: 116 123
Email: jo@samaritans.org

Selfharm UK

www.selfharm.co.uk

A project dedicated to supporting young people impacted by self-harm, providing a safe space to talk, ask any questions and be honest about what's going on in their life. They also provide guidance to parents and carers who are affected by self-harm.

Email: info@selfharm.co.uk

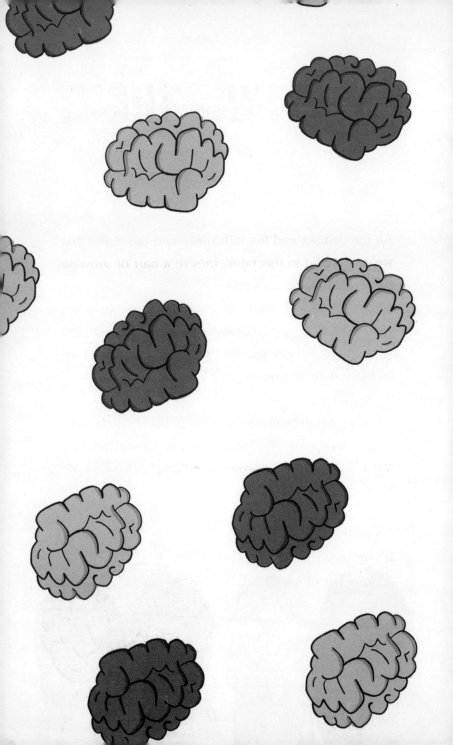

ONE FINAL THING

All the conflict and the difficulties and the stress that we've covered in this book, they're a part of growing up. It might take your brain a while, but it will sort out all the updates it needs and things will calm down. I can't promise any of you that your brain will then work perfectly forever, but whatever does happen, however difficult, you've got it covered.

Because that thing inside your skull? That wrinkly lump of grey custard is the most complicated and interesting thing in the known universe. (Although it's often the most annoying, too.)

Go easy on it.
It's unique,
a literal one of a kind.

It's you.